ROAD TRIPPIN

The Life and Times of a Comic on the Run

Jeff Hodge

iUniverse, Inc.
Bloomington

Road Trippin
The Life and Times of a Comic on the Run

Copyright © 2013 Jeff Hodge

iUniverse books may be ordered through booksellers or by contacting:

iUniverse
1663 Liberty Drive
Bloomington, IN 47403
www.iuniverse.com
1-800-Authors (1-800-288-4677)

ISBN: 978-1-4759-8282-4 (sc)
ISBN: 978-1-4759-8281-7 (e)

Printed in the United States of America

iUniverse rev. date: 4/29/2013

TO DONNA WOODARD-HAMILTON.

CONTENTS

FOREWORD

"Home"—what a lovely word. Brings up thoughts of relaxation, family, security, and good times. The opposite of home—the road. The nasty ole road. Most comics hate the road. But unfortunately, it's a necessary evil when you're a comic still working at reaching some measure of fame and fortune. You need that stage time, and the small clubs all across this country provide that. Stage time … that's what comics live for. Moments in the spotlight and a chance to let an audience show you some love.

Then again, the road's not all bad. When you're onstage and in that spotlight, the opposite sex tends to feel an attraction to you. That can lead to a different kind of performance. Plus, many people do treat you special. They put you on a pedestal. But … it's not home. You're not around family. It gets lonely. Jeff has experienced his share of all of the above and came out on top. Mellow and cool, he weaves his way through small towns, small clubs, obnoxious customers, celebrity hounds, and comedy condos and escapes the road unscathed. Still waiting for fame but enjoying the ride.

Bob Fisher
Owner of the Ice House Comedy Club in Pasadena, California

ACKNOWLEDGMENTS

Thanks   Tiffany Kinchen, Connie Griffin, Nathan Pinto, Jocelyn Pimentel, Marlene Harrison, Brandi Browne, Claudia Cruz, Sam Cox & "The Comedy Gym." Photos on the inside of the book were taken by Larry Davidson, Studio Wonderland, Madene StillBlessed, US military photographers, Michael "Franko" Franklin.

Special Thanks   My parents, Ruby Vanterpool, my brothers and sisters, the Ice House Comedy Club, Bob Fisher, B. Friedman, R. Kawamoto, Danny Martinez, Connie Griffin, Ashley Anderson, Khari Wyatt, Arnell White, Marlene Hunte, Deitra Kay Stevens, Paulette Hodge, the Comedy Workshop, the Comedy Showcase, Carol Phillips, Tricia Wilson, Jacqueline Campbell, Megan Davis, Rushion McDonald Arsenio Hall, Scott Atwell, Ken Harrison, Kristi Johnson, Khari Wyatt, Megan Davis. Chelsea Handler's book, *My Horizontal Life*, which was the blueprint for my book.

Acknowledgments   Denver "Spence" Williams, Francis "Big Fran" Acquaye, Kelvin "Jah Weeble" Hodge, Clarence "Claddy" Hodge, Edgar Hodge, Jr., Terence "TC" Hodge, Lauren "Ren" Gumbs,

Gerry Bednob, Dean Taylor, Daphne Hodge, Caroline Pope, Tina Strange, Vanessa Moise, Lori Shynell Sonnier-Guidry, Shelia Anderson-Dural, Marlene Harrison, Yvette Wood, Shirley Gumbs, Kristi "KJ" Johnson, Albert Linton, Henry Anderson, Twana Brown, Debra I. Hodge, Romona Carter, Marie Griffin, Nikki Williams, Beth Meyer, Alice Fuller, Jeffrey Hughes, Derek "Makim" Hodge, Glenn "Humpy" Taylor (RIP), Mike Jackson, Zefera Hodge, Jeffrey "Macho" Thompson, California Comedy Traffic School, Cedrick "Hollywood" Robinson, Donna Funchess-Smith, Jeff Donaldson, Brian Dennis, the Improv Comedy Clubs, Flappers Comedy Club, Barbara Holliday, L. Chantel Parma, M. Collins, S. Stephens, J. Ziegler, T. Riley, J. Perez, K. Cansino, M. Garcia, I. Sanchez, M. Andersen, K. Langhorn, A. Higgins, S. Carew, H. Bazil, L. Dunlap, D. Smith, B. Parson, M. McIver, J. Carcamo, M. Miller, J. Teemer, J. Siroonian, K. Langhorn, T. Roman, M. McIver.

Introduction

In the past two decades of my journey touring across the world doing stand-up comedy, many of the people I've encountered along the way have this idea that all comedians are out there chasing skirts when we're not onstage. Many even believe that we have a woman in every city where we perform. That is not always the case. For some comedians, that is true to some degree. However, the comedians with groupies all over the country have some kind of fame from their television or film appearances. The rest of us unknown comedians have to rely more on old-fashioned methods, such as our looks, charm, or just being funny.

Not all comedians are chasing skirts just to add notches to their belts. Some of us are searching for true love. Unfortunately, we may have gone about it the wrong way, but hey, at least we're trying. I know because I did. I decided to write this book to give my fans an inside view of my sex escapades while chasing the dream of being a famous, successful stand-up comedian and dealing with my demons as a sex addict.

Like most male performers, I love the attention from attractive women who approach me after one of my performances. I am a sucker for love. Like that old country song goes, "I keep looking for love in all the wrong places." I used to believe that all the problems I had finding love were not my fault and laid the blame on my female partners. As I look back, I realize that perhaps I was the problem. I was not good at sustaining a relationship. I would get caught up in the excitement of a new relationship and then a fear of commitment took over. Next thing you know, subconsciously, I was doing things to sabotage my relationship.

I have a high sex drive. Don't know if it's because I just like sex a lot or because my babysitter molested me when I was a kid. Lucky for me, my babysitter was a female, so I enjoy sex with women. I enjoy it so much that sometimes I think I have an addiction. I don't know if the addiction stems from the molestation or because I'm just a freak, but in the past it has definitely clouded my judgment when it comes to picking a girlfriend.

I noticed that whenever I gave ladies one of my comedy business cards and told them I was a comedian, they reacted to me more positively, as though they were intrigued by what I did. The seduction had already begun once I approached a woman, gave her a card, and invited her to a show. It was a great conversation starter because the ladies who were interested in me usually asked follow-up questions, such as "When is your next show?" "Where can I see you in action onstage?" "Are you funny?" Questions like those told me the woman doing the asking was interested in more than my show.

I am such a sucker for a stable relationship that the search for one has led me to heartbreak and setbacks. The loneliness of traveling on the road and performing has kept me on a constant search for true love. Sometimes I mistook lust for love—but hey, can't blame a guy for trying. My desire for someone to talk to during those many lonely nights in sparse hotel rooms and cookie-cutter comedy club condos wore on me. I told myself that if only I could have that one companion who could travel with me, someone who understood my character flaws and weaknesses, perhaps I wouldn't continue to torture myself day after day and week after week in search of that perfect relationship.

My buddy Big Fran would always tell me that I was the typical performer. He said I needed the adulation and attention and I was always chasing women because I was trying to keep that high going when I wasn't onstage. He would say, "Jeff, you need the attention like humans need oxygen. It's a character flaw that you couldn't correct if you wanted to." All performers have it. Mine just manifested itself in screwed-up dating habits in the pursuit of a relationship. Big Fran once said that when I finally found myself in a real relationship, I would probably sabotage it by going out and doing something stupid and destructive. He went on to say that when he first met me, he thought it was the women causing my relationship issues. After getting to know me for over a decade, he realized that I was the problem.

Some people may wonder why I wrote this book. I wrote it to share with my readers the inner turmoil we as comedians sometimes go through even though we're supposed to be happy people who are quick to make others laugh. Being a comedian has its good and bad points, but sometimes the bad shows up in destructive behavior that permeates our entire life. When things get bad or difficult for some comedians, they turn to drugs, alcohol, food and other vices. My demons have always been women. Getting up onstage in front of strangers is a tough job. Throw in the constant traveling around the country by yourself, the loneliness and empty feelings that seem to follow you from town to town once the laughter's gone and the lights turn off, and you have a recipe for disaster in many comedians' lives.

There's a reason I have never been married even though I've had opportunities. The real reason is because I enjoy the limelight too much. I feel as though I'm on top of the world when the club is packed and everyone in the audience is laughing with me. Unfortunately for me, I also like the things that go with being a comedian onstage—the adulation of the fans, mostly the admiration from my female fans. I thought it was best not to put someone else through the drama of my inability to control the urge for new companionship when that lonely, empty feeling snuck into my life. I have seen what happens when a love triangle forms. The breakup is never pretty. I guess that's why I kept the women I dated at a distance and tried not to get deeply involved. I didn't want to drag them down into my life of misery when my needs and insecurities reared their ugly heads.

Sometimes I felt like David Banner of *The Incredible Hulk*. David Banner was fine so long as he was calm, but when he got excited, he changed into the Incredible Hulk, and all hell broke loose. Then he was always on the move, trying to find that cure so he could rid himself of the creature buried within him. That was how I felt. As I've gotten older, I've been able to contain my demons more and more, but there have been times when the loneliness has crept in and that empty feeling came back—especially when I haven't been onstage for a while. I'd just freak out. Overall though, I have gotten better at holding back my destructive impulses. I have even gone to therapy to seek help for my problems, but as with any addiction, recovery happens one day at a time.

Before I get to the juicy stuff, let me share my evolution from being a teenager living in St. Thomas, US Virgin Islands, to living on the American mainland, chasing my dreams of being a comedy star. Most of the time when I had some kind of problem or drama in my life, it was usually with women and it wasn't always sexual. It's like this: when a woman doesn't understand a man's dream, the situation can cause more problems than anything else. It usually starts him off on the wrong path, the path of doubt — and for a performer, self-doubt is a lethal cocktail. It's the worst addiction and I was hooked before I even left home ...

Onstage performing at Club Gemini in Monterey, California. Fall 2004.

1

My Mother

St. Thomas, US Virgin Islands

I was fortunate to grow up in a two-parent home in a middle-class family in the Virgin Islands. I grew up in the 1970s, back when things on the Islands were very conservative. I grew up listening to Jimmy Cliff and a young Bob Marley on the radio. This was the period right when the new Jamaican music with the laid-back sound called ska was morphing into reggae. Jimmy Cliff was a much bigger star than Bob Marley at the time. I remember listening to Jimmy Cliff's songs on the radio, which were in heavy rotation on the two radio stations we had on St. Thomas. In 1972, Jimmy Cliff's movie, *The Harder They Come*, was released, and Jimmy became the hottest international star in the Caribbean. It would be many years before Bob Marley eclipsed him as the biggest international star from a third-world country. I grew up listening to reggae and calypso music, living a carefree life. R & B music played on the radio too, but only the more popular tunes out of America. Little did I know that these would be some of the best times of my life.

My dad was a no-nonsense kind of guy who had dual jobs as a contractor and a taxi driver. He drove a taxi most of the time and occasionally stopped to build houses. My dad was low-key and quiet. That was until he got to drinking or angry at one of his children for doing something they weren't supposed to. Then you couldn't shut him up.

On the other hand, my mother was just the opposite. Where my dad was quiet, my mom was very talkative. She was always talking on the phone. My siblings and I secretly nicknamed her "AT&T." Mom was more of a people person, whereas my dad was not. Mom was very affectionate, and again, Dad was not. Come to think of it, I have never seen my mom and dad kiss in my lifetime. My dad showed his emotions by being there and providing for his family. Now that I am grown, when it comes to showing my feelings, I see a lot of my dad in me. I keep a lot of the mushy-wushy stuff on the inside. To this day, my mom is still very sweet and religious. And such a wise woman, considering her education stopped at the junior high school level. I love her dearly and have called her many times as an adult to thank her for the guidance she gave me through my formative years. With that said, my mother was the first woman I clashed with in my life. The reasons varied, but she was always lecturing me about something, and I hated being lectured.

Growing up, like most kids, I used to think my mother didn't know what she was talking about. She used to have a saying for everything, and I always thought she was making them up. For example, whenever one of her kids would tell her they hated school, she would say, "Enjoy your school days because these are the best days of your life." I always thought, *Yeah, right. I can't wait to get out of school, get my own place, get married, and have sex every day.* Thirty years later, I realized how right my mother was. Getting up every day and working to make money to pay bills sucks. Also, I found out that getting married and having sex every day is a big myth. Now when I tell my kids to enjoy their school days, they give me the same crazy look I gave my mom back when I was growing up. If I could go back and live rent-free in my parents' home again and not have to worry about bills and buying food, I would do it in a heartbeat.

Another reason my mom and I clashed was church. Around age nine, I made the mistake of telling her that I hated going to church. Why did I do that? The minute I told her that, she was determined to make me go at any cost, and I was just as determined not to like it. It became a test of wills. I thought church was boring and told her so. She must have thought it was boring too because she never used to go either. I told her that and she gave me one of her signature backhanded slaps—the fastest backhand in the West.

We lived on the western part of St. Thomas, so we called it the West. She had four boys and two girls; my sisters were the babies. I was number two of six children. By the time my brothers and I got to a certain age, whippings from a belt were meaningless. They didn't even hurt. One day my mom overheard me telling my next-door neighbor this little fact, so she stopped using a belt and turned to her dreaded backhand. I learned fast that whenever she was interrogating me and started drifting closer, I should get ready to duck. She tried to backhand me into a church pew anytime there was service. It was bad enough having to go to church on Sundays, but night services were the worst. Talk about a cure for insomnia. Church never failed to put me to sleep.

To keep the peace in the house, I would go to church when my mother sent me, but my brothers and I started ditching service after we got there. My mom would send us to church with Mr. Gumbs, one of our neighbors who lived directly across from our house on the hill. Like my father, Mr. Gumbs was a taxi driver, but he didn't work on Sundays. My mother would procure a ride with him for all her kids to go to service, a service he would never fail to miss. We would go to the Sunday school classes and make sure that my aunt and my mother's other spies saw us there. Then when the main service started, my brothers and I would break out. Before we left, we would make sure that my little sisters knew to ride back home with Mr. Gumbs if he was going home after church. If not, we would make sure they knew where to catch the church bus. Then we'd take off and go exploring for the day.

There was a candy store near the church, so sometimes we would make a run to load up on candy before we started our journey. Sometimes we would go by the waterfront or stop by Griffith Park to hang out. Griffith Park was a rec center with a baseball field and basketball court. Occasionally I would go down there and shoot some hoops, or we would go down by the golf course, which was near our home. No matter what we did or where we went, we would make sure that we got home around the same time my sisters returned with Mr. Gumbs or the church bus.

To this day, whenever I speak to my mom on the phone, she always asks me if I've been to church. I always tell her yes, even if I haven't been in a while. She gets so excited when I tell her that I've been to church. This leads me to believe that if I told my mom that I won ten million dollars in the lottery and then turned around and told her that I went to church, she would get more excited about the latter. In my mom's defense, I'm glad she made me go to church back then because having faith in a higher power has helped me through some tough times over the years. For the record, my mother attends church all the time now.

My mom didn't take it too well when I told her I wanted to be a comedian. Because I made good grades and was an honor student in school, she thought I should pursue a career as a doctor, attorney, or some noble profession where the income was steady and lucrative. That was all good, but by my senior year in high school, I knew I wanted to be a comedian. I remember the first time I told her my career goals. We were talking on the phone, and she was asking me about attending college. I told her that I was thinking about skipping college to become a comedian. Being from a small island and not really knowing what I was talking about, my mother asked, "What is a comedian?"

"Someone who gets up onstage and tells jokes," I replied. So she said, "That's no way to make a living. You need to go to college because you'll need something to fall back on."

Without missing a beat, I said, "Okay, I'll buy a bed." Then I started laughing. In my head I thought that was a very good comeback.

There was a slight pause on my mother's end of the phone. Then I heard her say, "Jeffrey, that was not funny!" I knew she was upset because she called me by my full name.

I eventually enrolled at the University of Houston just to appease my mother and bide time until I could pursue stand-up comedy full time. After six years at the University of Houston, halfheartedly studying but mostly pursuing comedy gigs, I quit to perform comedy full time. For the next twenty years, my mother would harass me about going back to college to get my degree.

My mother never saw me perform stand-up comedy until 2002. Up until then, she'd tell her friends and coworkers that I was an actor. No matter how often I reminded her I did stand-up comedy, she would still turn around and tell people that I was an actor. At the same time, she was still hounding me about going back to school and finishing my degree, so finally I did. In 2004 I graduated from California State University, Northridge, getting my degree in Cinema-TV/Film. Even though my parents couldn't make it to my graduation, my mother was so proud of me. I remembered her asking me what I was going to do now that I had my degree. I told her that I was still going to do my comedy. Even though she had seen me perform live, she still didn't understand how I could make money at it. The way I finally got my mother to accept me doing stand-up comedy was by telling her I was doing the same thing as Bill Cosby. There was a long pause on her end of the phone. When she finally spoke, she said, "Well, if Bill Cosby is doing it, then it's okay." And that was that. After fighting the good fight for twenty years to get my mom to support my career choice, all it took was mentioning Bill Cosby, and all was well. I could have saved myself a lot of headaches and grief over the years if I had just dropped Dr. Cosby's name. Who knew?

Church and career were the causes of many battles, but the number one thing my mom and I knocked heads about was girls. See, my mother was very nosy. She had to know every and anything going on with her kids. I was just the opposite, trying to keep my stuff private. I remember an incident from the second grade. It was a sunny Sunday afternoon, and I was in my room thinking about this little cutie in my class named Betty. I liked Betty and wanted to know if she liked me too, so I wrote one of those notes we all wrote back then: "Dear Betty, I like you. Do you like me? Yes or no?" I folded up the little paper and put it in my shirt pocket. I forgot it was there until later in the afternoon, when I was passing by my mom and she happened to see a little piece of paper sticking out of my pocket. While she was asking me what it was, she took the note out of my shirt pocket, and proceeded to read it. She asked, "Who is Betty?" I told her Betty was a friend from class. To this day she still asks me, "How is Betty doing?"

I guess that was the moment when my mom discovered that girls were my thing, and after that she started watching me like a hawk, constantly warning me about leaving the girls alone and concentrating on my schoolwork. She said she didn't want to be a grandmother at such a young age. She didn't have a thing to worry about because I wasn't getting any sex back then. The only thing I was getting from the girls were good phone conversations, some hand holding, and an occasional kiss here and there. Girls weren't really putting out back then, at least not for me.

It's funny how things change when you become an adult. Now that I am a grown man, single, with two kids, my mom would like nothing better than for me to settle down. She keeps asking me if I can't find a good woman to marry and settle down with. My, my, my, all those years of telling me to leave the girls alone and study. Now she wants me to find a nice woman and settle down. She would get upset every time I showed up to a family reunion or event with a different female friend. It's gotten to the point now that when we're having a family event, she always tells me, "Don't show up here with any women." Most times I never listened to her, and she would always give me that wicked look only a mom can give. I just ignored her and tried not to let her catch me alone because I knew she was going to interrogate me about the lady of the moment: Who is she? What does she do? Has she ever been married? Does she have any kids? How many? Where did you meet her? All in all, I knew deep down she was probably hoping the woman she was meeting this time around was the one to finally make me settle down.

I have come to realize that moms are very protective of their sons, perhaps more so than dads. A father won't say much to a guy dating his daughter. He'll get his point across by showing the guy his gun (in the Islands, substitute gun with machete). Moms will actually confront the ladies dating their sons and occasionally mix it up with them if they don't like the woman. My mom has never mixed it up with any of my lady friends that I've introduced her to, but she has come back and told me things about the ones she didn't care for. I think what my mom failed to understand was just because I was dating these women, it didn't mean I planned to marry all of them. I guess she felt like I shouldn't be bringing them around if I wasn't willing to make a commitment. Some of them I did plan on marrying; things just didn't work out the way I wanted them to.

Onstage performing at The Improv in Hollywood, California in 2002.

2

WELCOME TO AMERICA

Houston, Texas

It was July 15, 1981, when I moved to Houston, Texas. In 1981, a lot of tragic events were happening around the world that would forever change our lives, but I was too young to even notice or care. The year 1981 was the same year Ronald Reagan was sworn in as the fortieth president of the United States on January 20, only to almost die by a failed assassination attempt on his life on March 30. Bob Marley lost his fight with brain cancer on May 11. An assassin wounded Pope John Paul II on May 14, and an Islamic assassin assassinated Anwar el-Sadat, the president of Egypt, during a military parade on October 6. All this turmoil was happening around me, but I was too busy being a teenager having fun. Bob Marley's death was the only event that took place in 1981 that really resonated with me. I was a teenager who grew up listening and dancing to his music, so I could readily identify with him, especially since he was from an island in the Caribbean too.

I was fifteen years old in 1981, and I was going to live with my aunt in Texas. My aunt, Sister Ruby, was one of my mom's older sisters. We called her Sister Ruby because she was a Christian, and that was what everyone called her at church. I started calling her Sister Ruby around the house, and all my family picked up on it, and it stuck. Sister Ruby had never been married and never had any kids of her own. She had moved to Houston a few years earlier and had decided to take in one child from each of her siblings and let them come live with her. I volunteered to go live with my aunt in Texas. I wanted to get away from St. Thomas for a while because I saw how moving away to live in the States had boosted a couple of my childhood friends' stature amongst the girls. My childhood friend Glenn "Humpy" Taylor moved to New York two years earlier and came back to visit a year later, and all the girls were all over him. Then my next running buddy, Derek "Makim" Hodge, moved to New Jersey a year later to live. When he came back to visit a year later, again the girls were all over him. Seeing how the girls received him when he came back to visit cemented my decision to get off the Island for a while. I was determined to get to Houston no matter what happened.

Still, I wasn't sure if my mom would really let me go, so my siblings and I didn't tell anyone in the neighborhood about my plan. A few days before I left, my mom came to me and explained to me that she wasn't sending me away because she didn't love me. She said she was only letting me go because I'd told her that I wanted to go. If I didn't want to go, she would call off the trip. I tried to tell her without seeming too anxious that I really did want to go. If I had to swim to Texas, I was going. I couldn't wait to leave little St. Thomas and head to big, bad Texas. I kept fantasizing about my new life in the States. I couldn't wait.

The morning of July 15 came and it was time to bounce. My mom and dad drove me to the airport to link up with my chaperone, Samuel Rymer. He was a family friend who grew up with my parents back in Tortola, British Virgin Islands. He was also the brother of my godmother, and he was already living in Texas. Matter of fact, he was the reason my aunt moved to Texas. He was our church pastor, and when he and his family left the Islands, they moved to Texas and extended an invitation to my aunt to come visit or stay if she ever wanted to get away from the Islands. My aunt was very old school, very religious, and was sort of an unofficial hostess and goodwill ambassador of our church. She pretty much stayed in church seven days a week. All my mother's siblings were like that. My dad's side of the family was not, so we didn't have to go to church all the time like my cousins. I think this is what gave me a balanced life of street smarts and a respect for a higher being, which kept me from going over the edge later in life, when I was faced with those dark moments.

Initially I was excited about leaving St. Thomas and heading to Texas, but when it was time to board the plane, things got tough. I didn't cry, but I damn sure wanted to. I don't recall either of my parents shedding tears, but I could tell they weren't happy to see me leave. It wasn't until I was on the plane heading to Puerto Rico that the gravity of the moment sank in. I was leaving everything that I had come to know for the last fifteen years and moving to a strange new place. For a minute there when we landed in Puerto Rico, I wanted to call my mother and tell her to come get me, but I didn't want to look like a punk. How could I face my buddies when they found out I was crying to come back home by the time I got to Puerto Rico? I figured I'd at least wait until I got to Texas before I made that call. Hey, what did I have to lose but a couple of days?

I made it to Houston, and the first thing I noticed when I stepped off the plane was how hot it was in Texas. St. Thomas was hot, but I swear I had never felt any heat like this before. I thought I turned a couple shades of black the first few hours I was in Houston — from brown skinned to midnight black. I also lost several pounds in water weight from the humidity. I made it to my aunt's apartment, where my two cousins, Tony and Angel, were waiting for me. They made me a homemade cake to commemorate my arrival. The apartment complex had a swimming pool, so I knew I was going to enjoy my stay in Houston. I figured I could wait until the end of summer to make that call to my mom telling her I wanted to come back home. Until then, it was time to let the fun begin.

Onstage performing at 29 Palms Marine Base in California, 2006.

3

MEXICAN HEAD

Houston, Texas

I worked at the Houston Astrodome my last two years in high school. This was right around the time when Michael Jackson's *Thriller* album was burning up the charts and winning him all kinds of music awards. Run-D.M.C. had just burst onto the music scene, and all the guys were bumping their cassette tapes in their cars. It was a thrill for me to get the job at the astrodome because I'd watched the Houston Astros' baseball games on TV growing up in St. Thomas; now here I was, working inside the astrodome.

I didn't have a car, so I used to catch the bus to and from work. I didn't mind — I was just glad to be working in the dome. I worked in one of the concession stands. My boss was an old lady whom everyone called Mrs. Tilly. She had to be in her sixties when I was there. Apparently, she had been there for almost twenty years. Mrs. Tilly treated me okay, but she could be mean at times. If you didn't agree with the way she wanted things done, watch out! I tried to stay out of her way whenever possible.

The concession stands in the dome weren't that big. There were approximately seven to eight workers that crowded into each station. Each person had a specific job. Two people worked on prepping the hot dogs. Another person worked on serving the soft drinks, another person poured beer from the keg, and we had two cashiers who worked out front. Mrs. Tilly guided proceedings from the back office and kept supplies plentiful. I worked the soft drink machine. It was boring, mindless work. I would always try to jazz up my job by engaging the customers in conversation and trying to make them laugh with a clever joke about the teams playing or the food. For example, whenever a customer ordered a soft drink with a mix of Coca-Cola and Sprite, I would tell them we called that a suicide, and as bad as the Houston Astros or Houston Oilers were, there was no need to end their life over the game. It always got a laugh.

Because Mrs. Tilly had been there for so long, the staff at her station usually stayed the same. She could pick and choose who she wanted to work with her. This was good and bad for a couple reasons. Good because since she liked me; I got to work whenever there was an event at the astrodome. Since it was seasonal work, that was very important to me. It was bad because I always had to work with the same old people all the time. There were hardly any new faces coming to work with us.

Then one day, one of the people who was prepping the hot dogs got sick, and she was replaced by a seventeen-year-old, sexy African American babe named Michelle. This girl was definitely a head turner. For the job, they gave us a company shirt that we wore for every event and turned in before we left the venue. Michelle strolled in there, company shirt stuck to her, wearing some chic jeans that showed all her curves in the right places. She had long, wavy hair and a pretty smile. I was so happy to see her because we were the only two people working in that stand who were under forty years of age. Naturally, we struck up a conversation. I found out that Michelle went to Willowridge High School, which was close to my high school, James Madison. For the next few months, Michelle was scheduled to work in the station with me, and I was a happy camper.

As the days passed and Michelle and I continued working together,

I noticed a couple things: she got lots of male attention, and she liked using guys for her benefit. When I saw this, I made sure to keep our relationship strictly on business terms. Lucky for me, I did, because things were about to come to a head. One day I was scheduled to be off and Michelle couldn't work for whatever reason, so she asked me to cover her shift. I wasn't doing anything, so I agreed to do it. She said that she would return the favor in the future. A month went by and I was scheduled to work, but there was a hot party going down that I wanted to attend. Michelle was scheduled to be off, so I asked her to cover for me. Without thinking about it, she just flat out said, "No!" I asked her why. "I don't want to," she replied. When I reminded her that she owed me a favor, she said she didn't owe me any favors, and if I didn't get out of her face, she was going to tell Mrs. Tilly that I was bothering her. Then she sauntered out of the concession stand and went to the restroom.

I couldn't believe what I'd just heard. I asked Michelle for a favor, and she just straight up flipped on me. I was hot, and I felt like kicking her ass, but I chilled. I vowed to myself that I would neither forget this day nor forget the incident. A few more weeks passed, and Michelle and I were back on speaking terms, but after seeing her true colors, I kept my distance. She must have sensed this because the next day she brought me some homemade cookies as a peace offering. When she wasn't looking, I threw those suckers away. No telling what she might have put in them. I noticed how Michelle operated. She knew she looked good, and a lot of guys liked her, so they would kiss her tail and bring her all kinds of gifts in hopes of scoring a date with her. I saw how she used some of them, and I wasn't about to let her play me like that. To make matters worse, she would brag to her girlfriends about her pimpish activities at the astrodome. It was a running joke between them.

One day, after I finished my shift, I was walking out to catch the bus home. Michelle asked me to wait for her because she needed to ask me for a favor. I wondered what she was scheming on, and I made sure to stay on the alert for any of her bullshit. When she finally caught up to me, she asked if I could switch shifts with her that upcoming weekend because she had to take her graduation pictures, and she wasn't sure if she would make it to work on time. I knew she was lying because I'd overheard her telling one of her girlfriends that she had a hot date the same night she was asking me to switch with her. I flat out told her, "No!" She looked shocked, and I knew it was because she wasn't used to hearing the word "no" come from a guy's mouth in response to her.

Then she asked me, "Why won't you switch with me?"

I said, "Because of that stunt you pulled on me a month back when I asked you to switch shifts with me."

She tried to explain away her behavior as PMS. "I was having a bad day," she said.

I told her I didn't care—I wasn't going to cover for her, and that was my final answer. Then I started on my way.

She ran up to me and screamed, "Guys don't walk away from me! I walk away from them!" I kept on stepping. The crazy girl tried to grab my arm, but I pulled away. Then she started calling me names! "You punk. You just mad because I won't go out with you! I would never go out with anyone who has a Mexican head!"

Now I've been called many names before, but being called a Mexican head was a first. I later found out that she was referring to me having a big, fat head. I used to get teased a lot back in elementary and junior high school about having a big ass head. At first it bothered me to no end, but then I got used to it and started accepting it. Finally I found a way to take the sting out of the put-down. Whenever someone said I had a big, fat head, I would simply respond, "So is the head in my pants!" It usually put a stop to the name-calling.

I could tell that leaving Michelle standing there in the parking lot was really getting to her. At one point she threatened to scream rape and get me arrested if I didn't come back and talk to her. I just kept walking and never looked back.

I heard she wound up working on the day she wanted off and that she was bad-mouthing me the entire shift, but I couldn't have cared less. She was nothing but trouble, and I kept my distance from her after that.

Onstage performing at The Ice House Comedy Club,
Stage 2, in Pasadena, California, 2012.

4

FUTURE HOMEMAKERS
OF AMERICA (FHA)

Houston, Texas

When I moved to Houston in 1981, I was entering the tenth grade. It was a new experience for me just learning my way around such a large city and meeting new people. My cousin Angel moved to Houston from Sumter, South Carolina, around the same time as I did, and he came to stay with my aunt and me. Angel was two years older than me with a very dark complexion. He was also a grade ahead of me, very personable, and outgoing. Everyone liked Angel. Girls loved his dark complexion and welcoming personality. To fill out his class schedule, Angel took a homemaking cooking class. Part of taking this class involved joining the club affiliated with it: Future Homemakers of America (FHA).

At first I was reluctant to join FHA because it was an organization mostly for girls that dealt with stuff guys weren't supposed to like. But one good thing about FHA was the presence of those girls—hundreds of them. So shortly after joining FHA, we started going on trips all over the country for area, state, and national meetings. The meetings were more like conventions because they usually lasted anywhere from a weekend for area meetings to an entire week for the national gatherings. Each meeting was usually in a different city. The area meetings encompassed the area surrounding the major cities in Texas. Normally over a thousand delegates attended these meetings. The state meetings were held in one of the major cities in Texas on an annual, rotating basis. State meetings averaged six thousand delegates. The national meetings were held in any major American city and averaged twenty-five hundred delegates. We always stayed at hotels when we attended one of those meetings, which were always fun because by day we did the meeting thing and by night we were free to play.

The best part of these FHA meetings was the unlimited supply of females. The ratio of girls to guys was always astronomical — like a hundred girls to every guy. There were girls of every shape, size, and color buzzing around me at those meetings. And because there were so few guys, those who were fortunate enough to be attending got to pick however many girls they wanted to talk to. Actually, we got picked up by the girls more often than the other way around. A lot of those girls were there to have fun just like some of us guys. Talk about a man's paradise. Many of my male classmates initially laughed at me when I told them I'd joined FHA. Then when I told them about all the girls I was meeting, the hotel stays, and all the traveling, they quit laughing and made a mad dash straight to Mrs. White, the chapter leader, trying to join FHA. Most of them couldn't get in, so they lived the FHA life vicariously through me.

Little did I know at the time, FHA was important to me because it turned out to be a training ground for my future occupation. A lot of skills I picked up — such as learning how to read a road map, how to travel from city to city, checking into hotels, interacting with large crowds and women on the road — served me well later in life as a touring comedian.

Onstage at The MBar in Hollywood, California in 2011.

5
The Houston Comedy Scene

Houston, Texas

It's not true that all comedians were class clowns. I was never a clown. Believe it or not, I was, and still am, a very shy person. I got into comedy kind of by accident and some curiosity. Like I said, I grew up in St. Thomas, US Virgin Islands, a small place where the population is about fifty thousand. When I was growing up in the 1970s, the culture in the Islands was very conservative. It still is, but a lot has changed in the Islands since the early 1980s. For example, when I was coming up in elementary and junior high school, it was unheard of for me to have a girlfriend and consider visiting her home or meeting her parents at such a young age. If I did, her dad probably would have chased me out of his house with a machete. When I got to America, things like having a girlfriend in junior high were commonplace. So when I say I didn't really know what a comedian was until I came to America, understand that a lot of that stuff wasn't popular in the Islands. People went to school or work, came home, and just relaxed on the weekends, whether on the beach or at some local gathering. All our television programming came from the United States or Puerto Rico, and we received only the most popular shows or cartoons. Until I moved to Houston, I wasn't up on a lot of the inside jokes and characters like the kids on the mainland were.

So when I was living in Houston, attending James Madison Senior High School, I was having a rough go at it. My classmates were laughing at me because of the way I talked. They would try to get me to speak just to hear my "funny accent." At times I felt like an exotic animal in a zoo when they surrounded me and tried to prod me into talking. It got so bad that I stopped speaking altogether when I was at school. Many days the thought ran through my mind to move back to St. Thomas.

Now, I have to say, the girls were nicer than the guys. Some of the girls said they admired my accent while the guys were just straight-up assholes. Somewhere in the latter part of my sophomore year, I figured out that I was talking too fast, so I slowed down a bit. More classmates started understanding me, and I began to gain more confidence and the friends that came with it. I was finally invited to various social activities by classmates and friends. It was in those settings that my peers first noticed my sense of humor and told me that I was funny. Some even suggested that I should become a comedian. Back in St. Thomas, the thought never ran through my mind, but after moving to Houston, that all changed. My newfound popularity brought it back.

By my senior year in 1983, I knew my way around Houston and had plenty of friends. Between the various FHA meetings and social activities I was attending, I started hearing more and more about how I should be onstage. That was right around the time when Eddie Murphy and Prince burst on the scene. Someone gave me a Richard Pryor comedy tape and told me to check it out. I started listening to Richard Pryor's act and memorized five minutes from it. Then right after graduation, I went down to the now closed Comedy Workshop on open mic night. I did my five minutes of Richard Pryor's act and completely bombed. I tried doing it one more time before I went home to visit my parents that June, and again, I bombed badly.

Bombing onstage is a terrible feeling. My stomach got twisted into knots, my mind went blank, and I could barely breathe. I so badly wanted to run offstage, but my legs wouldn't move. All that kept going through my mind was how I should've never listened to all those people who told me I was funny, and when I got off this stage, I was never going to get back onstage to try telling any more jokes. As you can see, I didn't follow that advice.

It would be another two years before I gave the comedy thing another go. I was sitting in an architecture class at the University of Houston daydreaming more than actually doing any classwork. I really didn't want to be there. My buddy Ashley "Ash" Anderson came up to me and asked me if I'd ever thought about becoming a comedian since I wasn't doing too well with the architecture thing. Ash was a tall, light-skinned brother from Houston. He had a calm demeanor about him and was a very good judge of character. I had never told anyone about my unsuccessful venture down at the Comedy Workshop. That day I confided in Ash that I had tried to do the comedy thing, and I wasn't funny, so off to college I went. I didn't really want to go to college, but my parents said I had to do something constructive with my life. My choices were either to join the US military or go to college. My older brother, Dell, who was already in the military, advised me not to join up, so I decided to give college a shot since I was an honor student in high school.

For the next month Ash worked on building my confidence and persuading me to give the stage another try. After he promised to help me, I agreed to it. I worked up five minutes of original, funny material, which Ashley and I remembered me saying around campus, and I went down to the Comedy Workshop on another open mic night. Right before I went onstage, Ash came up to me and said, "Hey, Jeff, it's real easy to make me laugh, so I don't know if you're funny. Good luck tonight though." My confidence and my five-minute set that night went right down the drain. I bombed again.

Eventually I figured out how to tell jokes onstage and make people laugh, thanks to a comedy class I took called the Comedy Gym in the summer of 1986. They taught me how to write, set up, and deliver a joke in front of an audience. Then I became a regular at the Comedy Showcase, a comedy club in south Houston, owned and operated by the extremely funny comedian Danny Martinez. It was at the Comedy Showcase that I finally developed my skill as a comedian, under the guidance of Danny and the club manager, the late Joe Grady.

I also became a regular at the Comedy Workshop right about the time I became a regular at the Comedy Showcase. The Comedy Workshop was much closer to my place and had many more open mic nights for new comics, so I worked there more. The problem with the Comedy Workshop was that the regular performers there were very cliquish, so when I first started going down there to work out material, none of the comics would talk to me. I wanted to fit in and be accepted, but they shunned me like the plague. So to keep that lonely, empty feeling away while I was waiting to go onstage, I would invite a couple of my buddies to come hang out with me whenever I got a spot.

My boys, such as Denver "Spence" Williams, Kenny "Jah Weeble" Hodge, and Clarence "Claddy" Hodge, would all come hang with me before my sets. Spence, my best friend, and I met in an acting class at the University of Houston. He was six feet tall, handsome, mellow and real cool. Jah Weeble is my youngest brother — he is two years younger than me and funny as heck. My mother always thought Jah Weeble would grow up to be a comedian. So did I, because he was always cracking me up. Claddy, a younger cousin of mine on my father's side of my family, was tall and wiry. Claddy would eventually become my wingman in the early stages of my career in Houston. These guys would all be with me in some capacity over the next two decades, cheering me on or encouraging me when the journey got too difficult.

The stage time at the Comedy Workshop was paying off: my comedy act was improving. I'd begun to understand how to work the stage and connect to the audience, and my sets were starting to rock the house. Little did I realize that my newfound powers would lead to perks I would find difficult to turn down.

Onstage at The MBar in Hollywood, California in 2011.

6

But You're Married

Houston, Texas

I was never one to mess with the staff at a comedy club. You know that old saying "Don't shit where you eat!" This is good in theory, but when you're in a strange town for up to a week and you have nothing but time to kill, as a comic you're going to find some way to stop the boredom. Another reason I didn't like messing around with the waitresses at the club was because if things went badly between the two of us, it could cost me a return booking at the club. Don't get me wrong, there was always a waitress or two at every club I performed in that I would've loved to hook up with, but usually I never took advantage of those opportunities.

Except once. Her name was Kelly. She worked at one of the biggest comedy clubs in Houston for many years. She was at least eight years older than me, and if memory serves me correctly, she was married at the time. Kelly and I became good friends from the many times I performed at the comedy club she worked in. When the club started a comedy defensive driving class, I became an instructor, and I would always see Kelly after teaching my classes at night. She usually worked every night the club was open because she had seniority. I found out later, after we started hooking up, that the main reason she worked so often was because she was a very unhappy housewife. Her husband worked for an oil company making good money, and she didn't have to work, but Kelly insisted on keeping a gig. She didn't want to be home with her hubby at night. She also liked the lifestyle of being around comedians and hanging out after the shows, eating, smoking, and drinking into the wee hours of the morning.

That's how Kelly and I wound up spending time together. I made it a point to never mess with married women, so I never looked at Kelly in a sexual way. I heard a lot of comics talk about wanting to sleep with her, but she was off-limits as far as I was concerned. Then one night after I finished teaching a comedy defensive driving class, I stopped by the showroom of the comedy club before going home. As I poked my head inside, Kelly saw me and came over. She asked me how long I was going to hang out, and I told her at least until the show was over. She told me she had some gossip to share, and she was going to see if she could get off early so we could grab a drink and talk. It sounded good to me.

After about fifteen minutes, Kelly told me she gave her tables to another waitress and that we could leave. We left the club and decided to drive up the street to a local dance joint. Since I really didn't drink much at that time, I was ordering Cokes and Sprites, and Kelly was ordering *real* drinks with alcohol. I was just hanging out with Kelly and, as we say in Texas, "shooting the shit." It never occurred to me to keep tabs on how many drinks Kelly was consuming. This would play a deciding factor in how the night would end. After a couple of hours spent sitting there talking, Kelly wanted to go to another one of her favorite bars close by. She knew the staff and could get free drinks there if the owner wasn't around.

We drove over to this bar, and immediately Kelly started knocking down the drinks. I was so naïve back then about people who drank, it never occurred to me that she was getting more inebriated by the hour. I do remember thinking that she liked to drink and smoke more than anybody I had been around. She insisted on buying me an alcoholic drink, so I told her to order me something sweet. Part of the reason I didn't drink back then was because I never knew the names of any alcoholic drinks, and I hated the taste of beer, so I stuck with what I knew—Coke and Sprite. If I wanted to mix it up and live on the wild side, I would have the bartender mix both a Coke and Sprite in the same glass with a splash of Ginger Ale.

After we closed the second bar down, I drove Kelly back to her car, which was parked in the lot outside the comedy club. It was cold that night, so she wasn't in any hurry to get out of my ride. We talked for a few minutes, and then a few minutes turned into half an hour. An hour later and we were still sitting there in my car talking. Even though I didn't have a day job to get up for the next day, I still wanted to get my ass home and go to bed. So I tried to cut the conversation off and tell Kelly to get in her car and go home.

Before I could get the words all the way out of my mouth, I heard what I thought was sniffling. It was dark, so I couldn't really see Kelly's face all that well. *Was she crying?* She sure was. Kelly was in full waterworks mode, crying and saying how I didn't think she was pretty and I didn't like her. I assured her that I thought she was pretty and that I did like her. She asked, "How come you never tried to hit on me?" I tried to explain that I never made a pass at her because she was married, and I was trying to be respectful of that. She took my hand and said, "So? You can still come on to me." Before this could register in my mind, she said, "I'm so wet." Being naïve and not really comprehending what she was getting at, I told her that if she was sweating she could roll her window down. She responded with, "I'm wet and I'm not wearing any underwear, Jeff!"

I took a big gulp of air and asked her, "What did you just say?" Without hesitating, she repeated what she had just said, and this time, she dared me to do something about it. I thought about what she had just said and wanted to get out and walk away. I really didn't want this to happen.

Before I could respond though, she had already taken my hand and placed it under her skirt. She wasn't lying — she was wet all right, very much so. I was replaying the last few minutes in my mind, trying to figure out her intentions, when she said, "If you really liked me, you would do me right here in your car." Yes, I was ridiculously naïve. The older me still laughs at the young and dumb version. Stuttering and stammering, I asked Kelly if she was drunk, and she admitted to being tipsy but said that had nothing to do with how she felt about me. She said that she had secretly admired me for months and wondered when I was going to make a move on her.

Believe me when I tell you that I was shocked. Now, I'm no angel, but I was trying to do the right thing and not disrespect Kelly's marriage or mess up our friendship. So I decided to talk my way out of the situation. The more I talked and tried to get out of the situation, the more I realized I wasn't going to win this battle. Kelly was drunk and couldn't drive home anyway. Because she was married, I couldn't take her home. The longer I sat there, the hornier we both got. Before long, my pants were pulled down to my ankles and Kelly had climbed onto me. Even though I couldn't help enjoying myself, inside I felt really bad about what I was doing. I felt terrible about messing around with Kelly, but I felt even worse for breaking my own code of ethics by getting involved with a married woman. Because of our body heat, the windows inside my car fogged up. We stayed there for the next few hours, playing with each other. Kelly eventually sobered up enough to drive herself home. I went home and fell into bed.

Onstage at The MBar in Hollywood, California in 2011.

7

ALFA ROMEO

Flagstaff, Arizona

I met Barbara my second time performing in Flagstaff. This was back in 1990, right around the time the hit sitcoms *Seinfeld* and *The Simpsons* debuted on network television. Barbara was hot with long blonde hair, big tits, and a pretty face. She had her own place, a good job, and drove an Alfa Romeo. I actually met her through a friend of a friend.

The first time I performed in Flagstaff, I hooked up with the girl who worked at the front desk of the hotel where I was staying. Her name was Angela. Angela was a cute brunette who went to Northern Arizona University. She was twenty-two, flirty, and carefree. We hit it off the minute I checked in. The strange thing about a lot of the white girls I hooked up with while touring was that their fathers always seemed to be racist. I can't tell you how many times I heard, "If my father knew I was sleeping with you, he would kill me!" Angela and I kept in contact with each other briefly. This was way back in the early 1990s, before the Internet and e-mail. We called each other a few times, and I sent her a few postcards, but then all that came to an end. I could never get in touch with her no matter what I tried, so I figured she'd met somebody and decided to move on. So Angela was long out of my mind when I booked my next date in Flagstaff.

I found out from a fellow comic that the producer of the show,

Tony T, was shady. He told me to be sure to get my money right after I stepped off the stage the night of the last show. This was one of my first few times going out on the road, and I was excited. I was just happy that someone was booking me. The average person doesn't realize how much comedians yearn to be loved and accepted by the fans, the booker, and their families, so anytime someone was willing to pay you to do what you loved doing, you felt like you were on top of the world. So I booked the Flagstaff gig six months after my last adventure there with Angela. The shows were set for Thursday through Saturday at the Monte Vista Hotel in the downtown area of the city. One of the first things you learned when you started going out on the road was that you always called the week before you did the gig to confirm that the gig was still on and you were still booked. So I called Tony T, and he confirmed that I was still booked for the gig. Right before I got off the phone with Tony T, he informed me that Angela's brother was looking for me and was planning to kick my ass for knocking up his sister and leaving her high and dry. Then he hung up the phone with a laugh. What an asshole. A lot of club bookers are sleazebags, and a lot of comedians secretly hate them, but we're forced to tolerate them because they're the gatekeepers to our livelihood.

You'd think Tony T would have called and informed me five months previously when he heard about this problem with Angela's brother, but no, he waited until a week before I was supposed to arrive back in town to tell me. At first I thought about cancelling the gig, but I really wanted to do it. It wasn't like a bunch of bookers were beating down my door to give me work. Then again, I wondered if he didn't have me mixed up with another comedian because I'd kept in touch with Angela for a couple months after I first returned home from Flagstaff. She never mentioned anything about being pregnant. Besides, we used protection, so I didn't see how the heck she could've gotten knocked up unless the condom broke or she used the "turkey baster technique." That's where a female removes the used condom from the trash, takes a turkey baster, extracts the semen from the condom and inserts it into her vagina in hopes of getting pregnant by the guy. This only happened to rich and famous guys, and I was neither, so I didn't know what was going on. The story sounded fishy to me, but my name was attached to it, so I had to find out what was going on. I figured I'd go do the gig and just be extra careful when I got to Flagstaff.

So I made the twenty-hour drive to Flagstaff in my Honda Accord — just me, my compilation cassettes, a thirty-two-ounce bottle of Mountain Dew, and a big bag of Cheetos. That was my routine when I went on the road. The closer I got to Flagstaff, the more the tension built. When I checked in at the Monte Vista I didn't see Angela behind the front desk. I chalked it up to her being off or no longer working there. That's another thing I learned early about working on the road: the turnover rate in the business is real high. The club booker who really liked you at a club and booked you may not be there in six months or a year later when you returned. That went for the owners, staff, clubs, etc. You just went, did the gig, and moved on. You tried not to get attached to anyone or any club. I wanted to ask the girl behind the desk if Angela was still working there, but I didn't want to raise any warning flags just in case everybody was looking for me. I just played it cool and went to my room. I couldn't wait until 8:00 p.m. that night when our show started. I didn't know the comic I was working with, but it didn't matter. We probably wouldn't work together again after this week.

Because it was a two-man show and I was the featured act, I went onstage first. I did my time and had a pretty good set. Then I introduced the headliner and went to the bar for a drink. While I was hanging out at the bar, one of the waitresses approached me and asked if I was married. The question took me by surprise, but in my short comedy career I had learned real quickly that whenever a woman asked a question like that, she was interested in you. I replied, "Why do you want to know?"

She said, "Because I have a friend that would like you."

I was blown away by her response. So I asked her how she knew her friend would like me. She told me that her friend liked guys who looked and dressed like me. Keep in mind that back in the day I used to dress like Crocket and Tubbs from the old *Miami Vice* television show from the 1980's. I would wear those white club suits with a colorful undershirt and socks to match. Women at the comedy clubs loved it. I used to get all types of women approaching me to ask if I could teach their husband or boyfriends how to dress. As a comedian, I was more into getting the Best Dressed Comic Award at the shows than the Funniest Person Award (there were never really any such awards at comedy clubs). A few waitresses at a few different clubs told me that I was the best-dressed comedian they had ever seen perform at their clubs. I felt so special after hearing that that I bought them all a drink.

So I turned back to this waitress and asked her if she was the pimp or the agent for her friend. She said, "No!" Then I asked her what her friend looked like. She said that she was pretty, with long blonde hair, big tits, a nice body, and her own place; was a manager at her job; and she drove an Alfa Romeo.

I said, "If she looks like that, why does she need you scouting out guys for her? She should be able to get any guy she wanted."

She said her friend was a really nice girl who was between boyfriends, and I seemed like a nice guy that she would enjoy hanging out with. She told me her friend's name was Barbara and where she worked. She said that if I was interested, she would be meeting her the next morning for coffee and that I should join them and see for myself what she really looked like. I told her I would meet them in the morning. She went back to serving her customers, and I went back to watching the end of the show. I was kind of curious and excited already. I couldn't believe her friend looked as good as she said she did and didn't have a man.

I got up early the next morning, considering I stayed up all night tossing and turning, trying to talk myself out of going to meet this chick. The last thing I needed to do was start another meaningless relationship that began and ended with sex. At one point I had actually decided not to go and meet the waitress and her friend, but then I convinced myself that the waitress's friend couldn't look as good as she said and I wouldn't like her anyway, so I told myself it was safe to go. I figured I'd go by Barbara's job a little earlier than our prearranged meeting time to see if I could get an early preview. If she didn't look as good as her friend said, I would just skip the meeting and go back to my room and sleep.

So I got to the place extra early. It was a bookstore/coffeehouse, and the joint was busy for so early in the morning. I walked around, looking at the name badge of every female employee, and couldn't find Barbara. There were a couple of ladies without name badges, but I was hoping none of them was Barbara, since they looked nothing like the woman the waitress had described. Just when I decided to cut my losses and leave, I ran into the waitress on my way out. I pretended like I had just gotten there. Suddenly, out of nowhere, walks this five-foot-seven blonde with the body I had been informed about. The waitress introduced us and told her that I was one of the comedians appearing at the Monte Vista that week. She was polite and said hi. The waitress was just coming by to pick something up from Barbara, so she wasn't staying. I decided to leave when she was leaving too. I invited Barbara to the show, and she said she might stop by later that night. After the waitress and I walked outside, she asked me if Barbara looked like what she described. I said, "Yes, but even better." Before she walked off, she said that she could tell Barbara liked me, and it was up to me to close the deal. Then she left. I didn't get any vibes that Barbara was interested in me, but I figured I would soon find out.

I went about the daily routine I followed when I was on the road: wake up around noon, go to the mall, and hang out. Eat, come back to the room, watch a little television, and take a nap. I would go over my act a bit and tweak any jokes that needed reworking. That day, I couldn't wait until show time. All I could think about was Barbara. I had already forgotten that drama surrounding Angela. Matter of fact, I hadn't even seen her since I'd hit town.

Eight o'clock came and it was show time. When I got down to the showroom, the place was packed, and Barbara was front and center. I went onstage and killed during my set. Afterward Barbara found me at the bar and gave me a big hug. She felt and smelled so good up against me that I didn't want to let her go. She told me that she'd loved my set and thought I was hilarious. As she was telling me this, she handed me a tequila shot. We had a few drinks at the Monte Vista. Then Barbara, the waitress, the headliner, and I went to another bar. Because Flagstaff was a small college town, some of the audience from the show was there, so they started buying us drinks. Every so often, Barbara would ask me to do a shot with her, and even though I still wasn't a big drinker, I obliged and knocked down a tequila shot. As the night went on, I noticed Barbara getting cozy with me. She started kissing me and grinding on me every chance she got. Local guys kept coming in and seeing Barbara at the bar. They kept trying to talk to her while she was hanging with us. They would buy her drinks, and she would quickly pass them to me. When they found out that she was with the only black guy in the club, they would order both of us drinks. When the bar shut down, Barbara told me that she was taking me home with her. When she said this, I froze for a moment because I knew where it was heading if I went home with her. At first I tried to get out of it by telling Barbara my head was spinning and I didn't think I could drive. She countered by telling me I could ride home with her. Without saying a word, she put her arms around me and started walking me out.

It was cold as ice outside and snow covered the ground, so the Alfa Romeo was sliding all over the place. As we drove to Barbara's house, I prayed that nothing would happen between us. I hoped she would say that since we'd just met and she didn't really know me, I would have to sleep on the couch. I was really praying that Barbara would do something to torpedo the rest of the night, because I was just about out of willpower after drinking so many shots of tequila.

Boy, was I wrong. When we arrived at her place, Barbara and I pretty much tore each other's clothes off before the door even closed. We went at it a few times before finally passing out for the night. Some people say dog owners start to take on the look and characteristics of their pet. Well, Barbara was just like her car. Beautifully designed, stylish, and she handled well.

Barbara and I were inseparable for the rest of the week. She was a really cool lady. I learned that she had a ten-year-old son, but he was with his dad for the weekend. That Saturday we drove down to Sedona, Arizona, for the day before my show later that evening. I had never been there before. She showed me around the area and told me about the people who lived there. On the way down to Sedona, we had sex, and then she gave me some road head on the way back up to Flagstaff. She was a total freak in bed. I liked that about her; she was so uninhibited. We made love properly when we got back to her place — no rush at all, just slow and thorough, enjoying each other's bodies. She came to my show again that night, and we all hung out again after the show. Barbara had me drinking tequila shots again — she was the first person to ever get me to drink tequila. I didn't too much care for the taste — it was bitter and it burned going down — but in small doses I was willing so long as it kept Barbara open.

By closing time, I was a little buzzed. I went to the bathroom, and while I was in there, Barbara snuck in. We ended up damn near breaking down one of the stalls in the restroom. I was really digging Barbara. We went back to her house and kept the love flowing for the rest of the night. When we woke up it was Sunday, and I was scheduled to go back to Houston since the gig was over. I was having such a great time hanging with Barbara that I stayed for another week. She was incredible to me. She cooked me breakfast and dinner every day and gave me the keys to her car and her place. She would come home every day for a lunch quickie. It was hard to leave, but I returned to Houston the following Sunday. Barbara and I did keep in touch. Every time I went back to perform in Flagstaff, I stayed with her. I would actually go several days before the gig and stay for several days after. We always had serious fun when I was in town.

Onstage at The MBar in Hollywood, California in 2011.

8

Hunted

Galveston, Texas

Sometimes when a man thinks he's the hunter, he ends up being the hunted. In the early nineties, I was still living in Houston, and I was gung ho about getting stage time. I was doing any sets I could get. Around that time, one of my buddies, Albert "Big Al" Linton, called and invited me to go to an open mic night with him and some other comics in Galveston, Texas. Big Al was tall, dark, and one of the funniest comics I had met up to that point. He was always hustling for work. I think that's why we got along so well. There was no pay for this particular gig, but I decided to go along for the ride. Things weren't going so great between my girlfriend and me, so I needed to get out of the house for a minute and clear my head.

My girlfriend at the time only liked having sex once a month, and I needed it at least three times a day, so this created a lot of tension in our relationship. I was contemplating leaving her because I stayed sexually frustrated. As a result, that lonely, empty feeling had started to wash over me, and I needed some action. When that craving for attention and connection came over me, I threw all reason out the window and started taking all kinds of risks. I should have known something crazy was going to go down after I got that feeling, but I was constantly lying to myself, saying I had my problem under control.

I figured the camaraderie of riding to Galveston with Big Al and the other comedians and then performing would help fill the void.

I don't remember how many comics came along on that trip, but I do remember that we all drove down in Celeste's big Chevy Suburban. Celeste was Big Al's new squeeze, and she was driving that Suburban long before SUVs became trendy in the new millennium. While everyone was busy engaged in various conversations, I just sat in the back staring out the window, lost in my own tortured thoughts. The longer the drive became, the more I realized that I had lost the zest to perform. As much as I loved the stage, open mic nights were good for giving comics bad surprises. I was feeling restless, and a fifty-fifty proposition for success that night was not giving me the energy I needed.

The drive to Galveston from Houston usually took thirty minutes with a few miles per hour over the speed limit. But Celeste, lost in conversation with Big Al, drove like we were going to a funeral. I should have known it would be this way because Big Al was the same guy who made his ex-wife sit in his traffic school class for eight long hours on a Sunday to get her certificate for a speeding ticket. To this day, Big Al wonders why she divorced him. Another nickname for Big Al was "By-the-Book Al."

We finally got to Galveston after what felt like a week, and we went straight into the club. It was really a sports bar filled with a bunch of college kids on spring break. I walked into this place, and I immediately started regretting that I said I would perform. I have a way of being temperamental like that. If I was in character and feeling it, then I was in full party mode. However, if something was troubling me, watch out, you're going to get old man grumpy. I always did wear my emotions on my sleeve.

While we waited for the show to start, Big Al, Celeste, and I struck up a conversation. Then the other comics joined us, including Steve Bosco. Steve was sort of a clown/comedian, and he was emceeing the show. He was a short, stubby, Caucasian comedian who was a bit older than the rest of us. He had a wife and a kid and appeared to be happy with his life. This was something that was rare to find in the comedy business. Most of the married comics I knew or worked with were always cheating on their spouses. Eventually, Steve told me when I was going up, so I started walking around the place to get a feel for it. I wondered how we were going to do comedy in this place because the music was loud and all the people were talking just as loudly, shooting pool, and drinking. I was wondering to myself who would care about a comedy show?

Just when I was about to write the night off as a comedy disaster, I spotted this cute, hot chick coming down the stairs. She was holding a pool stick in her hand, and she was walking in my direction. She was kind of staring at me the whole time with a big smile on her face. At first I thought she was coming to talk to me. Then it hit me that she was probably going to the bathroom. Another thing I learned early in my career was that the best place to pick up chicks at the comedy club was near the bathroom. After sitting in the showroom laughing, eating, and drinking for a couple hours, sooner or later they had to go to the bathroom. If you had already performed and they thought you were funny, they would always speak to you. Then it was up to you to close the deal.

So as this blonde with the pretty smile and ample bosom walked by, I said, "Hi."

Not only did she say hi back, but she actually stopped to introduce herself. "I'm Monica." She asked me what I was doing there. This being a sports bar in Galveston, there weren't too many brothers hanging out that evening. Actually, Big Al and I were the only two black guys in the place that night. I came up performing in the white comedy clubs, so I was used to being "the only one" whenever I performed.

I told Monica I was a comedian and that I was performing that night. She seemed quite interested. She asked me if I was funny. I said, "Of course I'm funny." She replied, "Good, 'cause I like funny." Then she went to the bathroom. On her way back upstairs, she asked me when I was going onstage. I told her, and she said that she would definitely watch my set. Talk about being stoked and ready to go drop some funny on that crowd.

I went up onstage and did well. When I got off, Monica came up to me and told me she loved my set. We started conversing and I learned that she was from Lawrence, Kansas. She and some friends from the University of Kansas were in Galveston for the week on spring break. They were staying in a time-share that her grandparents owned on a private beach on the western part of the island. She asked me if I wanted to hang out with them for the week. I could tell she was down for some action because when she asked me, she got in my face so close that our noses were touching. She leaned against me and said, "If you don't have a girlfriend or a curfew, you can come back with us to the condo and spend the night." I was blown away, but I tried not to let her know I was dying to get in her thong. I found out later that thongs were all she ever wore.

Now I had a problem: I didn't drive my car to the club, and it was thirty minutes back to Houston. There was no way I was going to hang out with Monica and her friends without my car. I told Monica that I rode with the other comics and that I had to go back to Houston to get my ride. She told me that they would be staying at the bar until it closed at 2:00 a.m. By now the show was over, and the other comics were standing around chatting. I went and told Big Al and Celeste that I had to get back to Houston ASAP 'cause I had a meeting early in the morning. It took them a while to finish their drinks, but eventually, we all climbed into the Suburban and headed back to Houston.

The drive back to Houston seemed to take a month. The comics were all busy talking about their sets. I was busy looking at my watch, hoping like hell Monica and her friends didn't leave before I got back down to Galveston. I was looking forward to playing with those double

Ds all night long. We finally made it back to Houston, and as they dropped me off at my car, Big Al wanted to stay and chat a minute. I pretended I was tired, said good night, jumped in my car, and headed for Galveston.

Five minutes into my drive, I pulled off the freeway and into the parking lot of a fast-food restaurant. I started banging my head on the steering wheel and cursing at myself for doing what I was about to do. I was supposed to be going home, but here I was, chasing tail after another show, again. I'd thought I had this problem licked, but my old demons were rearing their heads once more. On top of everything else, I was starting to feel guilty because I should've been going home to my girlfriend, but I knew she wasn't going to want to mess around with me. I was horny as heck. My girlfriend hated sex and I loved sex. I think I stayed with her because she looked real good, but as long as I was with her, I was sexually frustrated.

I stayed in that parking lot trying to decide what to do for another few minutes. Part of me kept urging me to go home and forgo the excitement that awaited me in Galveston. The other part of me told me to go for it. Eventually excitement won out over morality. I knew I'd regret this decision tomorrow morning, but tonight I was like an addict, and I needed a fix big time.

I must have broken every land speed record from Houston to Galveston trying to get back to the bar before it closed. Keep in mind that this was in the early 1990s; way before cell phones and pagers became popular. As I pulled up to the club, I noticed the parking lot was empty, so I parked and ran in. As I ran in, I bumped into Monica and her two friends leaving. They were the last patrons to go. She said she thought I wasn't coming back, so they were finally leaving. Monica rode with me, and her friends (her two friends were a couple) followed us back to the condo in a separate car.

As many times as I had been to Galveston, I had never gone to that private beach. As we got inside the condo, we all got something to drink. I wasn't much of a drinker back then, so I had a wine cooler while Monica and her friends were drinking beer. As we all sat there chitchatting, Monica snuggled up to me as if to let me know she was ready for some action whenever I was ready. We sat around talking for an hour and then we split off into pairs. Me being the anal-retentive person I am, I was taking off my clothes and folding them up neatly, but before I could completely finish folding my clothes up, Monica had already turned the lights out, stripped down naked, and started giving me oral favors. We ended up getting it on for the rest of the night. She was so good. Monica enjoyed sex a lot, unlike my girlfriend at the time, who preferred to have sex once month. That was way too infrequent for me.

The next morning, I felt real bad about not going home. While Monica was in the shower, I contemplated sneaking out. I felt one of those pounding headaches coming on. My stomach got real tight and I started to have an anxiety attack. *How was I going to face my girlfriend? What was I going to tell her?* I contemplated crashing my car instead of making that call to my ex. I figured if I was in an accident and ended up in the hospital, she might have sympathy for me and overlook my transgressions.

Finally I decided it was time to stop living a lie and call it quits between my girl and me when I got back to Houston. The way I was treating her wasn't fair to either of us, and I couldn't keep torturing myself like this. If I kept this up, I was going to die of a heart attack. The stress was killing me. I managed to pull myself together just in time before Monica came out of the restroom.

Monica and I hung tight for the rest of that week, enjoying each other inside and outside of the bedroom. As the week proceeded, I started to believe she liked sex more than me. We were doing it everywhere as frequently as I could get hard. One night after a gig at the Comedy Showcase in Pasadena, Texas, Monica and I were heading back to Galveston on Interstate 45. We had a thirty-minute drive and it was foggy as hell. I could barely see past the hood of my car as I sat behind the wheel, doing my best to see the road and keep us alive. Without saying a word, Monica leaned over and started giving me road head. I was trying to keep the car on the road, and here she was going down on me. Blow jobs are cool, but most of the women I'd been with up to that point couldn't seem to give me a happy ending while doing it. So it was usually a warm-up for me before starting the main event. But Monica was special—she always gave me the happiest endings. I think that's why I liked her so much. I almost ran off the road when I climaxed. It took everything in me to hold the car straight and keep us off the stairway to heaven that night. Damn, Monica was great in bed. I wished she was my girlfriend living in Texas and not the fling traveling home to Kansas.

As the week went by I learned quite a bit about Monica. She was a senior at the University of Kansas and would be graduating that May. Her mother used to be the mayor of Lawrence. Her family was poor, but they were loving and open-minded. The one thing she told me that week that stayed with me to this very day was that she was the one who actually hit on me and not the other way around. At first I didn't believe her, but she changed my mind when she put it this way: "I saw you while I was shooting pool, and I told my friend, "I'm going down there to pick that guy up and sleep with him." When she first told me that, I was shocked. Then I felt cheap. I couldn't believe how easy it was for her to pick me up. Oh well, she was hot, so I felt like a winner.

Monica was serious about really being with me and marrying me. She came to visit for a few weeks later that summer, and we had a great time. Even though we only spent a few weeks together, the sex was so good that I seriously contemplated something more. That's the thing about me: it's hard to break down my walls and make me fall in love, but if I like you and hang out with you a lot, I tend to get attached. Then it becomes very difficult for me to move on. In the end, Monica and I ended up going our separate ways because she found out about my live-in girlfriend.

Onstage at The MBar in Hollywood, California in 2011.

9

SHE SAID WHAT

Tulsa, Oklahoma

I got booked to perform two weeks in Oklahoma later in 1990. The first week I worked in Oklahoma City, the second in Tulsa. Danny Martinez was headlining both weeks, so I rode up with him. Danny was the owner of the Comedy Showcase in Pasadena, Texas (which is in south Houston). He was a funny guy who commanded a lot of respect in the Houston comedy scene. It was a nine-hour drive to Oklahoma City from Houston, so I figured I'd get some good stories and tips from Danny on the drive up there. Danny was a road veteran, so he didn't need me to help him drive. He could drive forever without stopping to pee. One thing I remembered learning during that road trip with Danny was that all the years he'd been doing comedy, he'd never cheated on his wife.

The first week in Oklahoma City was cool. We performed at a club named Jokers. I had performed in hotels and bars, but this was my first time performing outside of Texas in a real comedy club, and I was really jazzed up. The shows were packed, and the people were really friendly, especially the women. I had a blast. We finished the week on Sunday night and headed to Tulsa Monday morning. On the trip to Tulsa, Danny told me that the owner of the comedy clubs in Oklahoma City and Tulsa was one and the same. He lived in Dallas and he was super cheap. Because we were staying in a two-room condo, the club owner would be sleeping on the couch for the first couple of nights, and then he would head back to Dallas Thursday morning. It's bad enough we comedians have to spend the week with other comedians who are pretty much strangers to us every time we perform in a new city, but to have a club owner camp out for a few nights was not cool.

The first two nights in Tulsa, Danny and I did the shows, went and got something to eat after the shows, and hung out as late as we could until we thought the club owner had fallen asleep on the couch. Then we would come in, go straight to our rooms, and call it a night. The messed-up thing was that the only TV in the condo was in the living room where the cheap-ass owner was sleeping, so we couldn't even watch TV those first few nights.

After the owner left that Thursday morning, Danny and I felt more relaxed. We started hanging out in the living room watching TV after our shows. Most comedy clubs usually have two shows on Friday and Saturday nights. So by the time we arrived for the first show Friday night, it was packed but not a sellout. As we waited around for the second show, we could see that this one was going to sell out. I took the stage and started doing my thing. Five minutes into my set, three ladies walked in late. It was bad enough they were late, but they proceeded to cause a commotion by sitting up front. So I started cracking jokes on them.

After my set, I went and hung out by the bar. While I was standing there making small talk, this older lady walked up to me and said, "You were pretty funny."

I replied, "Thank you."

Then she said, "My daughter wants to fuck you!"

At first, I wasn't sure I heard what I heard, so I said, "What did you say?"

She said it louder. "My daughter wants to fuck you!" I was shocked, but I didn't want her to know this, so I covered by asking who her daughter was. She said, "We were the three ladies who came in late during your show. You talked about us and included us in your act."

Normally when you have a mother picking up guys for her daughter, you automatically think the daughter can't be too good-looking. So then I got down to real business and asked what her daughter looked like. She replied, "She was the pretty one on the end sitting next to me. I'll go get her."

I really didn't remember what she looked like. The picture that kept coming to mind was that of an older lady. I worried that perhaps this woman was trying to pass off the old lady who'd sat beside her as her daughter. Just when I was about to run for cover, the lady burst out of the showroom with this pretty young woman with long, jet-black hair and a break-your-heart smile. Mom walked up to me and introduced us. "Jeff, this is Tiffany. Tiffany, this is Jeff." Then Mom left and went back inside the showroom. Tiffany and I chatted through the rest of the headliner's set.

I learned during our little chat fest that she was a single mom with two kids and wanted to hang with me later that evening, but first she had to go and take her kids to their grandmother's house and then she could play. She would drive over to where I was staying. I really didn't know the address of the place we were staying, so I gave Tiffany the number to the condo and told her to call me there. I would give her the address then. After the show, Danny and I got something to eat and headed back to the condo. While he was in his room changing, I called Tiffany and gave her the details. She said that it would take her a couple hours to get there because she had to wait until the kids fell asleep. That was cool with me because I had to make sure Danny was asleep in his room before she got there. I didn't want him to see me bringing in some tail on our very first road trip together. I worried he might think poorly of me and never take me on the road with him again. So we sat there eating our food, watching TV, and shooting the breeze. I was also keeping a close watch on the clock. After about two hours, Danny didn't seem like he was going to bed anytime soon, so I started faking like I was sleepy. Then I told him I was going to bed. I went in my room, turned off the lights, and lay in my bed listening for him to turn in. About thirty minutes after I went to bed, Danny called it a night.

Within twenty minutes of Danny retiring, Tiffany showed up. As I was letting her in, she tried to talk to me, but I put my finger to my lips, gesturing for her to be quiet. Once we got to my room, I told her that I didn't want to wake up the other comedian. She told me she could stay the whole night. I was glad too because I wanted a serious piece of her ass. We stripped naked and got to sucking and boning each other for the better part of the night. After a couple of hours, we eventually fell asleep.

I woke up that morning around six for two reasons. One reason was so I could get her out of there before Danny woke up. But my main reason was because I wanted another crack at her in bed. That stuff was good, and just in case I didn't see her again, I wanted to make sure I got my fill of her. She had it going on! I almost told her to stick around for another hour so we could do it again, but I didn't want to risk Danny waking up and finding her there.

Later, when Danny woke up and we were hanging out before the show, he asked me if I'd had someone over the previous night because he thought he'd heard some voices. I told him he'd probably heard me talking on the phone. Tiffany called me during the day to let me know she was going to come see me after she got off work later that Saturday night. Because we had two shows, I told her that by the time she got off and came by, we should be done and back at the condo. Like clockwork, she showed up around twelve thirty, and we went at it again. She got out of there around seven that morning.

We had one more show Sunday night, an early show. We did the show, collected our money, and headed back to the condo. Because we were driving back the next day, Danny turned in early. I called Tiffany and she came right over. We didn't do too much talking when we got together that night. I guess we knew our time was short, so we just got down to business. The three nights that I hung out with Tiffany, I learned that she was a divorcée. Her ex-husband had treated her badly, but she had held on to the things that made her the cool chick she was: a lot of personality and a curiosity about life. When I went back to Houston, we stayed in touch via mail or phone. The next few times I performed in Tulsa, Tiffany and I would rekindle our sex escapades.

Onstage at The MBar in Hollywood, California in 2011.

10

LOVE TRIANGLE

Oklahoma City, Oklahoma

I used to perform in Oklahoma City about every six months. I liked the town, but this was approximately six months after the terrorist bombing in downtown Oklahoma City in 1995. I was a little scared about coming back to perform so soon after the bombing, but I figured it was safe. Besides, the crowds were always good to me. This was my second time working in OKC, and I was performing at Jokers again, once more as the opening act. The money was okay but nothing to write home about. However, I was just happy the booker liked me enough to bring me back.

I made the nine-hour drive from Houston to Oklahoma City and was glad when I finally arrived. I was happier to be getting out of my car because I had no air-conditioning at the time, and it was summertime sticky. At this point in my life, comedy was starting to wear on me. I hated taking these long rides by myself. I wished I could afford to pay one of my buddies to come on these road trips with me. The loneliness was starting to get to me. I found myself looking forward to meeting new people the minute I drove into a new town or city. So I made it to my destination in one piece.

I exited my car and went inside the condo. The feature act for the week, Ed, was already there. He was a nice guy from Ohio. He showed me where my room was, and I already didn't like the setup. To get to my room, I had to walk through his room. There was no way around that. For the entire week, I would pass by his room and see him in some state of undress or entertaining guests because that was the only way I could get into my room. The only other way to get in and out was to climb through the window. I wasn't about to do that unless it was a dire emergency, like some crazy chick trying to kill my ass with a knife while I was in my bed and she was blocking the doorway. Already I'd started to think this would be a crappy week.

I went outside to unload my stuff from the car, and I heard this butter-soft, sexy voice say, "Are you one of the jokesters?" I looked up and I saw this pretty, five-foot-two-inch Latina with shimmering black hair. It was just as hot in Oklahoma City as it was in Texas, and she dressed like it. She was wearing a pair of Daisy Duke cutoff shorts and a little halter-top.

I was already smitten by her looks so I said, "Yes, I am, and who are you?"

She said, "My name is Josefina. What's yours?" I stopped packing so I could go upstairs and introduce myself properly. We stood there talking for about an hour. I told her that I'd be performing at the club all week, and I wanted her to come check me out. She stared at me for a brief second, full of seduction, and whispered, "I'll think about it." Apparently she'd been living there long enough to notice this was the place the comedy club stashed its comics when they came into town.

I went back downstairs and finished unpacking my car. I could tell from Josefina's curiosity that we would be doing the horizontal tango before the week was out. I didn't know exactly which day it would take place, but I knew it was going to happen. Sometimes, a man just knows these things, especially when he's performing on the road.

The booking was the standard Tuesday through Sunday gig. Josefina and I would chat every time we saw each other during the week. She worked at a small law firm. Because she worked a nine-to-five job, whenever she was coming home from work, we were usually getting ready to go to the club to perform. Therefore, she said she would attend the weekend show. As the week went by, we grew closer. I would tell her about the previous night's show, and she would tell me about her day at work. She even invited me up for an early dinner one night before show time.

Saturday night rolled around, and Josefina informed me that she was going to attend the late show. Well, a funny thing happened that day. Last time I performed in Oklahoma, the feature act was a female comedienne/magician named Tracey. Tracey had a friend named Sunshine who lived in Norman, Oklahoma, who came to see her perform in Tulsa, and I met her. Sunshine told me to let her know when I was coming back to OKC so she could come and see me perform. So on my way up to OKC, I called and let Sunshine know that I was going to be in OKC that week. Guess what? While I was in town, Sunshine called and told me she was planning to come to the late show Saturday night too. I wasn't sure, but I had a strong feeling that Sunshine was feeling me.

The late show Saturday was on hand, and Josefina pretty much rolled up with me to the club. When we got there, Sunshine was already waiting. For the record, Sunshine was a six-foot Amazon of a blonde, with long hair past her shoulders. She spoke the language of sexual innuendo with a smoky voice that belonged on quiet storm radio. She was more sexy than beautiful, but no man would think of kicking her out of his bed. I introduced her to Josefina, and immediately I sensed an attitude between the two of them. Yeah, I thought, ole Sunshine did like me. It was setting up to be a long night, and I was going to need some help.

I got a table for Sunshine and Josefina and bought them a round of drinks, hoping it would take the edge off. Then I gladly went onstage to do my act. When I finished, I went back to the table with my female friends. I noticed the tension had doubled from the time I left them alone at the table. Of the two ladies, I was more attracted to Josefina, but Sunshine was more direct and vulgar when it came to saying what she liked sexually. Like I said, there was always sexual innuendo flowing out of her mouth.

So the show ended, and the ladies both started telling me they wanted to hang out. Now that I knew without a doubt that Miss Sunshine liked me, I needed a wingman to keep her occupied while I tried to close the deal with Josefina. I could tell Josefina was really digging me because since she'd seen my show, she'd been trying to stick exceptionally close to me. Every time I came around the table, Josefina would make it a point to tell me how funny I was and give me a well-placed kiss. It was as if she was marking her property. I think Sunshine sensed this, because her face flushed red with anger and her lips curled into a snarl every time Josefina would pull her little routine.

The feature act, Ed, was a homebody. He reminded me of Al Bundy from the old FOX sitcom *Married with Children*. He would pretty much do his show and go back to the condo to watch TV. He was friendly but not into the ladies as much as some of the other comics I'd worked with. So I grabbed Ed and quickly brought him up to speed on what was going down. I told him that I needed him to roll with us after the show or else I would be a dead man walking. Ed was a stand-up dude, and he agreed to go to the club with us and be my wingman for the rest of the evening. We went out drinking and dancing after our shows were over. I tried to trade off dancing with Sunshine and then Josefina, but every time I got up and danced with Sunshine, she would dog Josefina out. "Where did you find that tramp from? She isn't anything but a cock tease! She probably has some kind of STD. Let's ditch the bitch and go back to your place, blah, blah, blah."

I guess Josefina sensed that she was getting to Sunshine, so she started flirting with me harder than ever. I tried to play it off like I wasn't enjoying it, but Sunshine wasn't buying it. To be honest, if Sunshine wasn't there, I would've escorted Josefina into the bathroom and done her good right there. Ed was just sitting back, cool and easy, watching my drama unfold. Periodically he'd try to distract Sunshine, but she wasn't having any of that. Then Sunshine raised the stakes. She finally said that she was ready to go. Shit-or-get-off-the-pot time was at hand. We drove back to the comedy club where Sunshine's car was parked. I had already made arrangements with Josefina for us to meet down in my room at the condo. Because the comedy club was pretty much within walking distance of the condo, Josefina hopped out of the car and said that she would walk back to the condo with Ed. Just before she left, Josefina got one last dig in at Sunshine. She said to me, "I'll see you later, Mr. Handsome." Then she planted a lingering kiss on my lips and strolled away with Ed.

I pretty much had to hold Sunshine back from going after Josefina. Without warning, Sunshine then turned to me and asked me point blank, "Who are you going to fuck tonight? Me or that slut you came to the show with?" Now I'm a regular guy, and I won't even lie and tell you I didn't want a piece of Sunshine because I did, but I didn't see how I was going to make it work. Josefina was due to come by the condo any minute, so I couldn't take Sunshine back to my room. She kept insisting on going back to my place if we did mess around. After I saw that she wasn't going to go for us making out in the car, I made up some lame excuse about how I had to drive back to Houston real early the next morning because I had an important meeting to attend. That was a standard excuse I used back in the day, and it always worked.

Sunshine seemed a bit skeptical at first, but she pressed her case one more time, saying to me, "You're going to be missing out on the best piece of ass in Oklahoma. You sure you don't want to change your mind?" When she said that, I got so hard that I could have cut diamonds with my erection. I almost took her back to the condo with me to find out, but I knew I probably wouldn't get any ass that night because Josefina would show up and they would get into a screaming match. I'd probably be left there holding myself after they both ran out on me. I politely declined, asked for a rain check, and helped her into her car and watched her speed off. I could tell she was angry, but hey, what was I to do?

I ran back to the condo, Josefina came down, and I tore that ass up that night. Throughout the night she kept sneaking out questions about Sunshine, asking me if we had anything going on. I ignored all of that foolishness and kept her more than occupied. I gave it to her every which way that night. The next morning she complained about her "fuzzy triangle" being sore. I told her, "I humbly apologize, but that's the price you pay to have me to yourself." That seemed to turn her on, because she gave me one more go-around right then and there.

The sex was great, but when Josefina and I were finished and she went back upstairs, I was left feeling empty on the inside. I hated feeling that way, but it was the price I had to pay to temporarily relieve the loneliness that comes with traveling around the country by one's self.

Looking back now, I'm glad I picked Josefina over Sunshine because the next few times I went back to OKC to perform, she was ready and waiting for a brother. This went on for a couple of years, until I switched over to performing at the other new comedy club in Oklahoma City, The Comedy Corner. By then, Josefina had started an affair with her boss, who was an attorney and married. The last time I spoke to her, she was pregnant by him. We lost contact after that.

Onstage performing in my show, The Caribbean Comedy Tour, at Jays Place 2 in Stone Mountain, Georgia, 2011.

11
TWIN SMOKE

Lock Haven, Pennsylvania

When I became a comedian and first started touring on the road, I was so green and naïve. Looking back now at the places I've been and the people I encountered along my journey, I know I had an angel looking out for me every step of the way. The gigs and towns were starting to run together and so were the women I met. It was all starting to wear on me. I remembered having a long conversation with myself before going out on the road regarding not sleeping with anyone I met on certain road trips. I genuinely wished I could find a girlfriend I could take with me on all my tours, but because this wasn't possible, I did the next best thing: I found someone to comfort me when that lonely void came over me. It got to the point where some of the women I was with didn't even turn me on, but hey, if it meant conversation and company till the next day while I was in a strange town, I would take it. Alcohol has a way of dulling your sense of morals.

This reminds me of the time I performed in Lock Haven, Pennsylvania. It was a one-nighter. You know, the kind of gig they have at a local venue in some chump -change town once a week. You drive into town, do the gig, and the next night you're on the road to the next episode. Like most comics, I wanted to play the big rooms in the big cities, but until I could break into those venues, I took the gigs I could get.

So I got booked to do this gig in Lock Haven, Pennsylvania. It was part of a three-week string of one-nighters in the Pennsylvania – Ohio area. The gig before the Lock Haven one, I worked with another black comic. This was notable because back in the early 1990s, it was very unlikely to see more than one black comedian on the bill. A few years later, Def Comedy Jam would change all that, but this was before the Def Comedy Jam era. So I was working with this black comedian, and we were talking about where our next gig was. When I told him I was performing in Lock Haven, he looked at me like I was crazy and told me to be careful because rumor had it they still had signs up in the center of the town that read, "Niggers not allowed!" At first I thought he was joking, but I could see he was serious. He said the booker had offered him the gig, but he'd turned it down specifically for that reason. His last words to me before he left that evening were, "Watch your back!"

The night before the gig in Lock Haven, I experienced the worst night's sleep I had in my life up to that point. I was in a cold sweat, heart pounding, and stomach dropping. I was shaken and stirred. I kept tossing and turning, wondering if I should cancel the gig. I knew if I cancelled at that late date, the booker would get pissed and never book me again. I had never experienced racism until I came to America. I used to see movies and old footage of the civil rights movement on television, but that was another world to me. The times I did experience racism in America, sometimes it was so subtle that I didn't notice it until after the fact.

Sometime around three o'clock in the morning, I decided that I was going to soldier on and do the gig. I didn't usually check in every day with my family when I was on the road, but I decided I would call home when I got to Lock Haven and let my family know where I was. I'd tell them exactly where I was performing and who the booker was so that if anything happened to me, they'd know where to send the police. It might sound like I went overboard, but a comedian's life on the road was made up of many out-of-the-way towns where it was easy to disappear without a trace.

The next day I rolled into Lock Haven around midday. Our itinerary called for us to go straight to the motel and check in. Then we were to call the club to check in with the manager. I paid close attention to the people at the front desk as they were checking me in, trying to read their expressions. Turns out the clerks weren't that friendly. They were just business as usual. Our motel was on the outskirts of town, so after I checked in, I kept a low profile and stayed in my room. I grabbed something to eat and ate in my room so I didn't have to venture out to get anything. Since I hadn't slept much the previous night, I pretty much fell asleep the minute I hit the bed.

When I woke up it was already getting dark, so I showered, ironed my clothes, and went over my notes for that evening's show. Showtime was at nine o'clock, so I left around seven thirty. I didn't want to get there too early because I hated standing around waiting for a show to start. Before I left my room to go to the show, I called a few family members and friends and told them that I was leaving to go to the club. They wished me luck and told me to check in when I got back to my room. When I stepped outside, it was deep-space black. There were no streetlights where the motel was located, which only amplified my fears and anxieties about being there. For a fleeting moment, I considered not going, but I decided I wasn't going to let some ignorant racist keep me from making my money. I told myself that when I got to the club, if anything looked out of order, I would turn around and come back to my room and barricade myself in there until the next morning. So for fifteen minutes, I drove in utter darkness. The only lights visible were my headlights. It was like being in a slasher film, and I was the brother who would be the first to die in the movie. I was too damn nervous. As I drove over to the club, all kinds of crazy stuff kept going through my head. I wondered if anyone would call me a nigger and, if they did, how I would react. I'd never been in that position before, so I began having flashbacks of the movie *Mississippi Burning*, and I became more and more nauseated the closer I got to the club.

When I hit the city limits, there were more lights, and I found the club with no problems. When I pulled up to the club, I sat in my car a while and watched the patrons come and go. I had a really dark tint on my car windows, so I didn't worry about anyone seeing me. Since the area around the front door was poorly lit, I couldn't see the faces of the people going in, but I could hear some of their conversations. They sounded pretty cool. I decided that I would go in and check out the scene on the inside. But before I got out of my car, I remembered that I had a switchblade in my glove box, so I took it out and placed it in my pocket just in case. I entered the club very stealth like and stood close to the door to observe the goings-on. All I knew about Lock Haven was that it was a college town and the club normally had a good turnout for the shows.

As I was standing there getting a feel for the place, I noticed a black guy working behind the bar. At first I thought I was seeing things, so I focused my eyes, and sure enough, it was a brother making drinks. When I got to the bar I introduced myself and told him that I was one of the comedians for the night's show. He seemed excited to meet me. He stuck his hand out and told me his name was Frank. Then he told me the headliner had already arrived and was in the sound booth with the deejay going over his sound cues. Frank asked me if I wanted something to drink. I got my usual, Sprite on the rocks.

Frank made my drink and then called the club manager over and introduced us. His name was Joey. Joey was a forty-something, frumpy white guy with a friendly personality. He asked me if everything was okay with my room over at the motel and if there was anything I needed before I went onstage. I told him no. Then he informed me that one of the deejays from a local radio station was going to go up before me and open the show with some giveaways, tell a couple jokes, and then bring me up. I gave him my introduction to give to the emcee. He then told me that the show was going to start in ten minutes.

I looked at my watch and saw it was almost nine o'clock, so I sat on a stool by the bar and checked out the audience as they interacted before the show. The headliner came over and introduced himself to me as Alvin, from Florida. We kicked it for a few minutes about the business, motel rooms, the commute, and all the mindless things comics talk about when they initially meet each other out on the road.

The show started, and the radio deejay went up and did his thing. He was onstage for at least ten minutes. He gave away a few promotional T-shirts and music CDs and told a couple of old jokes. Then he introduced me. I always got a little nervous when I performed in a room for the first time, and this night was no exception ... until I got that first laugh, and then it was off to the races. I did my thirty minutes and got offstage. I had a good set, and the audience gave me an extended applause. As I stood around watching the headliner do his thing, I wondered why I had been so concerned about performing in this club. They loved me. I was starting to doubt there were any racist signs in this town — the people seemed too friendly. People from the audience were walking up to me saying how much they loved my set.

Because this was a nightclub, after the comedy show the club turned back into a dance joint. I liked those kinds of shows because many times after a show, I was wired and couldn't sleep. The clubs that turned into dancing rooms were ideal because I loved to dance and could work up a sweat. Another reason I liked the comedy show / nightclub format was because it was easier to meet ladies. Because the ladies had seen me perform, if they liked me, they would come up to me and let me know. This night turned out to be no different. Within twenty minutes of the show being over, there were four lovely ladies standing in front of me offering to buy me a drink. I just ordered Cokes and Sprites, but one young lady in particular refused to spend her money just buying me a Sprite. Her name was Trudi. Trudi was of medium height, with long legs and short black hair, and had a super friendly energy. She said I needed to order something with alcohol in it. I tried telling Trudi that I didn't really drink, but she wasn't having any of that. So I told her the few times that I did drink, I preferred drinks that were sweet. She said, "Then I have the perfect drink for you."

The next time the waitress passed by, Trudi ordered an Alabama Slammer for me. She said that I would love it. The waitress didn't take long to come back with my drink. It was red and in a big glass with a straw. I took a test sip, and it tasted good — like Kool-Aid with alcohol in it. In the Islands, we called it rum punch. So I took a few more big sips. The more I sipped, the more I drank. The more I drank, the more I talked. Trudi and the other three ladies were chatting me up. I could tell they all liked me from how friendly they were being. When the other three found out I was drinking alcohol, they all just had to buy me Alabama Slammers too.

I finished the one Trudi bought for me, and the waitress brought me another one. As I started sipping on my new drink, I asked the girls if it was true there were derogatory signs about black people still posted around town. The ladies all stopped drinking their drinks and looked at me nervously. One of the ladies blurted out, "Yeah, some crazy old guy has a stupid sign up in his yard saying dumb stuff about black people. They can't do anything about it because of his right to freedom of speech. Most people just stay away from him because he's crazy."

I said, "Okay, I understand." Their answer really calmed my fears about racism in the town, so I started letting my guard down even more. The conversation soon turned to my marital status and the question of whether I had a girlfriend. From my experience, whenever a lady asked a guy about his marital status, she was usually interested in him romantically in some way or the other. Just then, two really sexy-looking redheads walked up and asked me if they could speak to me privately for a minute. The question really piqued my interest, but I didn't want to just get up and leave Trudi and the other ladies, so I said, "Cool. Give me a few minutes." They quietly walked off and sat at a table close by. I continued my conversation with Trudi and the girls while occasionally sneaking a glance at the twins sitting there waiting for me. They would wave at me whenever I looked over at them. After a few more minutes of talking with Trudi and the others, I excused myself and went over to see what the redheaded twins wanted from me.

When I got to the table, the twins introduced themselves. Their names were Jennifer and Jessica. They were both very flirty and attended college there in Lock Haven. Jennifer said, "We saw your show and thought you were very funny."

Jessica continued, "How would you like to go back to our room, smoke some weed, and have a threesome with us?" The question caught me so off guard that I was at a loss for words. When I regained my composure, I asked them if they were serious. They both said, "Yes." And I do mean both said yes at the same time, as if it came from the mouth of one person. I checked both of the ladies' faces to see if they were joking with me, but they were dead serious. As if to prove to me how serious they were, Jessica and Jennifer each took one of my hands and led them under the table and up under their skirts. They weren't wearing any panties and I could feel the dew in the grass. My heart skipped a couple of beats just thinking about my good fortune.

Without removing my hand, I asked the ladies, "Why me? All these guys here in the club and y'all want to go back to the room and have a threesome with me."

Jessica replied, "Because you seem like you're a really cool guy."

Then Jennifer chimed in, "Besides, you're from the Islands. I've heard that Island guys like to smoke weed and they're fun in bed. Is that true?"

I said, "Yes, ma'am, but I don't smoke weed."

The minute I said that, Jessica and Jennifer's demeanor changed from flirty to cold. "What do you mean you don't smoke weed?" Jessica asked. "I thought you were from the Islands. Don't all Island people smoke weed?"

I said, "Nope. I have never smoked the stuff a day in my life."

Almost as if they had planned it together, Jessica and Jennifer reached under the table and quickly removed my hands from their femininity. Then they both grabbed their purses and stood up. Before they walked off, Jennifer got right up in my face and said, "Too bad you don't smoke weed. You could've had a lot of fun with the two of us tonight." Then they walked out of the club. I just stood there dumbfounded, watching their asses swishing back and forth as they walked away.

I was sort of relieved when nothing happened between the twins and me because I was fighting with my demons. I made a mental note to work harder on saying no and avoiding situations that led to the bedroom. I knew that was going to be a tough promise to keep.

Onstage in the Middle East entertaining the troops
at a US military base in Qatar in 2005.

12

CAN YOU HEAR ME NOW?

Corpus Christi, Texas

I was the feature act at a comedy club in Corpus Christi, Texas, and I was halfway into my act when I noticed a cute blonde sitting on the right side of the stage, continually whispering to her friend. After noticing this little exchange take place for a few more minutes, I finally asked the two ladies what was so important that they had to keep whispering to each other during my act. Again, the cute blonde whispered something to the older lady. Then the older lady whispered something back to the cute blonde. Then Blondie laughed. It was almost time for me to get offstage anyway, so I didn't get to lay it to them. I just wrapped up my set and got offstage.

As was my custom, when I got offstage, I went out into the lobby and got myself a drink. As I was standing at the bar sipping my drink, out walked Blondie from the showroom. She walked straight up to me, shook my hand, and said, "You're a funny guy. I like funny guys. You married?"

I looked around to make sure she was talking to me. "Why do you want to know if I'm married or not?" I asked as I turned to the bartender to order another drink. Just then, Blondie draped her hands on my cheeks and snapped my head back around so I was directly facing her. With the speed she moved, I thought she was going to break my neck. I quickly put my hands on her hands, removed them, and asked her why she did that.

She said, "Because I'm deaf and read lips. I couldn't see what you were saying with your head turned away from me."

I told her that I didn't believe her.

She said, "That was why my friend and I kept whispering to each other while you were onstage. I couldn't see what you were saying when you turned your back to my side of the stage, so my friend would repeat what you said." Blondie was a nice-looking, slender lady with voluptuous breasts. You could tell that she worked out from the muscle tone of her body.

I introduced myself and asked Blondie what her name was. She said, "Joanne." I told her I was going to call her Blondie. She said she didn't care what I called her so long as I bought her a drink. I ordered a Cape Cod for Blondie and we continued our conversation.

As I was standing there looking Blondie over, her friend came out of the showroom looking for her. Blondie's friend was short, pudgy, and a few years older than her. She was sporting a short hairstyle and was average looking at best. She spoke to Blondie briefly and walked back into the showroom once she knew she was okay. Now I have a bad tendency to look around when I'm talking, so during my little chat fest with Blondie at the bar, she kept twisting my head back to her so she could read my lips. At first it wasn't a problem, but after thirty minutes of all that twisting, it started hurting. However, I was willing to endure a little pain if it meant getting some bedtime with Blondie. As we chatted, I learned she was born with the ability to hear but lost it in a car accident when she was young.

I heard the headliner doing his closing bit and told Blondie the show was about to end. She wanted to go out dancing after, so I asked her how she was going to go dancing when she couldn't hear the music. Blondie responded by saying, "I can feel the vibrations and I move to it." She said she knew of a club close by, so I said fine.

When the show ended, Blondie's friend came out looking for her again. Blondie told her that she was going to hang out with me for a while. After she repeatedly reassured her friend that she would be fine, her friend left us alone. They'd driven to the show in separate cars, so that wasn't a problem.

The club was within walking distance, and during our walk over to it, she kept telling me to turn my head and repeat myself because she couldn't see my lips. By the time we got to the club, I felt like a broken record.

The minute we walked into the club, Blondie became another person. She got more aggressive and started grabbing and feeling on me. Like most dance clubs, it was dark and loud. We danced a few times, but I could sense that Blondie was horny and down for some real action. I pulled her aside and asked her if she wanted to go back to my room for a drink or two. I made sure I was looking right at her when I asked her because I didn't feel like repeating myself. Without saying a word, Blondie grabbed my hand, grabbed her purse, and led me right out the front entrance of the club. My hotel was within walking distance of the club, so we held hands all the way back to my room, talking and laughing.

When we got back to my room, I tried to make Blondie a drink, but she was more interested in getting down to business. We started kissing. At the same time, I started unbuttoning her blouse and she started talking to me, asking me questions about herself, such as, "Do you think I'm attractive?" "Do you like me?" Do you like my breasts?" "You think they are big enough?" I didn't mind the questions; the thing that bothered me the most was that after she asked a question, she would literally pull me away from what I was doing to her or about to do to her, grab my head, and turn it to her face so she could see what my answer was. After the fourth time she snapped my head up from her nipples, I stood up and told her that I couldn't go through with our plans. Her neck-snapping ways were a mood killer. As much as I wanted a piece of Blondie, I didn't think it was worth risking decapitation to have sex with her. Besides, my neck was killing me from her constantly grabbing my head and yanking it.

Blondie protested and promised not to do it again for the rest of the night, but I was no longer in the mood. My head throbbed and I just wanted some sleep. At one point she offered me oral and said all I had to do was lie there and she would do all the work. I just crawled into my bed and turned off the lights. Blondie saw that I was in pain and was nice enough to give me two Excedrin tablets with a glass of water. I downed the pills and lay back in the bed with the pillow over my head. After what seemed like forever, I finally fell asleep. I slept till noon the next day. When I woke up, my headache was gone and so was Blondie.

I was upset with myself the next day because I'd fallen into my same old habit of turning to a female fan to fill that void I can't seem to shake when I'm out on the road. By default, nothing happened, but if my head hadn't started hurting, I would've been beating myself up for going through with another night of meaningless sex. I considered quitting comedy and just settling down with the first chick who said she liked me when I got back to Houston, but I didn't think that would solve the problem. I considered turning to recreational drugs to numb my mind and the emptiness I felt when I was on the road, but drugs weren't my thing. I didn't know the first place to go to buy any kind of drugs except the pharmacy, and that was no good. I didn't feel like I could talk to any of my friends about my issue because I was afraid they would laugh at me and tell me to man up. What was I going to do? I had to find a cure for my problem because I didn't want this to be a factor in any future relationship of mine. I wanted to be a one-woman man, but I was losing this battle. I brainstormed all through my five-hour drive back to Houston. There had to be a way to shake this monster.

Denver "Spence" Williams and I emceeing our show,
The How To Keep A Man Comedy Jam, at HaHa Comedy
Club in North Hollywood, California in 2006.

13

SO ROUGH, SO TOUGH

Houston, Texas

I remember one time I went back to Houston to visit family. It was the week of my thirty-fifth birthday, and I scheduled a week of shows at the Laff Spot, a comedy club in North Houston right off of FM 1960 and 249 Road. A Houston comedian named Don Learned owned it. Whenever I wanted to visit my family, I always tried to book a club to help offset my travel expenses. The club owner booked me as the feature act that week. The money was just okay because it barely covered my travel expenses to and from LA, but I didn't care. I was back in my old stomping ground. It's funny, whenever you moved to LA or New York to live as a performer, all your friends treated you like royalty when you went back to visit. They thought you were in LA hanging out with celebrities every day. They just didn't know how wrong they were.

So I was in Houston hanging with friends and performing at the club all week. The crowds were light in the early part of the week, but the shows were going fine, and I was having fun. My thirty-fifth birthday was coming up fast — it was the Monday after my last show that week. One thing about being a performer, half of the thrill of performing was winning the pretty girls over. I always liked it when I had a good show and made the audience laugh. It was even more special when the pretty ladies came up to me after a show and told me how funny they thought I was. It was almost like the woman was coming up to me, telling me that she wanted to sleep with me. Man, what a feeling. The downside to that was when you're a sex addict and you're trying to fight your demons, the constant temptations put you in direct conflict with your own self.

Sunday night came, the last show of the week, and I was ready to pull out all the stops. As I started my act, I noticed a guy sitting up front with two ladies. After messing with them and making them part of my act, I learned that he was with one of the women, and the other was just a friend of theirs. Apparently she came along just for the laughs. Periodically, I would come back and mess with this group. However, something told me that the lady without a date was interested in me. She was cute — a thick white chick with sandy brown hair and bright hazel eyes. I decided to find out for sure when I got offstage.

I finished my act and went back to the office to get paid. One thing about being a comedian was you always made sure you got your money as soon as the gig was over, or you might not get what was owed to you. On my way out of the office I saw Ms. Hazel Eyes and introduced myself. Her name was Karen. She and I talked for a minute and my assumption was correct. She'd come to the show by herself and was trying to find something to do later. I told her I was game for anything, and she suggested we meet at a sports bar on the south side of town, off of Interstate 10 and Beltway 8. I was glad she picked that area because I was staying with my brother, Jah Weeble, and he lived in Missouri City, which was in southwest Houston.

I considered driving straight home and skipping meeting up with Karen. I prayed part of the way on my drive over to the sports bar, asking the Lord to give me strength to go straight home. At one point I was certain I was going to drive past the bar, but I caught a light right where the bar was, and after sitting there waiting for the light to change, the lure of the excitement to come won out. *Here we go again*, I remember thinking as I got out of my car.

We met up at the sports bar, and she seemed to be a regular there because she knew all the workers. I bought a couple rounds of drinks, and we got to know each other even more. After about an hour, Karen asked me if I wanted to get a room. I was DFW —down for whatever! I was in town visiting and I had plenty of time to kill. Now I knew it was wild living, and I wouldn't advise anybody to go to bed with perfect strangers, but it was what it was. Being a performer opened up a Pandora's box that was hard to close at times. There was a motel just up the street from the sports bar, so we went there; neither one of us wasted any time dropping our clothes. I enjoyed myself, and I guess she did too because she said she was ready for round two. While we lay there waiting for my second wind to kick in, we got to talking. Karen asked if my birthday really was the next day. I said, "Yes." She said her birthday gift to me would be for me to wake up inside her. I wasn't planning to stay the whole night, but since she put it that way, I was willing to oblige.

During the night of our sexathon Karen kept telling me that I didn't have to be a gentleman with her coochie—she had born two kids through it, and it was okay if I wanted to get rough with it. I can't speak for other guys, but I was never into the rough stuff. If there was pain involved, I didn't want any part of it. She kept urging me to get rough with her but I couldn't do it. Still, I ended up hitting it a few more times before we parted ways.

Karen had given me her number, and I had given her my pager number. She called me during the day to wish me a happy birthday. Then she asked me if I had any plans for my birthday that evening. I let her know I was free, so she insisted on taking me out for dinner and then giving me dessert afterward. We met around eight at Pappadeaux Seafood Kitchen somewhere on Westheimer Road, a strip of bars, clubs, and restaurants that were popular in the Houston area. The dinner and conversation were good, but we both knew we were just putting off what we really wanted to do, which was screw each other to sleep. We didn't even wait for the rest of our meal to come out. We told the waitress to box it up, and we got it to go. Then we hurried back to the same motel from the previous night and got into some serious lovemaking. When morning came she left before me, and I left at checkout time. Karen said she was going to call me later in the day, but she never did. I found that quite interesting because the previous day she'd called me a couple times before I had even checked out of the motel. I did talk to her later in the day, but she sounded distant. I asked her if I was going to see her later, and she told me she'd be at the sports bar that evening.

Later that evening, I went by the sports bar and saw Karen sitting at the bar talking to some guy. I walked up to the bar, greeted her, and ordered a drink. Karen grudgingly said hi to me but continued talking to her male friend. I asked her if there was a problem between us. She interrupted her conversation long enough to tell me no and then continued talking to her male friend. I got the feeling that something was going on between them, but I didn't want to start tripping; I mean, after all, Karen wasn't my woman. So I just sat there sipping my drink for a few minutes. After about ten minutes, I asked Karen if I could speak to her privately for a minute. She agreed and we got up and walked outside.

When we got outside, I asked her what the hell was going on. Why was she acting the way she was, and who was the guy she was with? She told me he was an old flame, and he was hanging with her for the night. She said that she was into rough sex and I wasn't cutting it for her. She'd tried to get me to rough her up in the bed like she liked it, but I'd refused, so she was done with me. She turned, walked back into the bar, and left me standing in the parking lot like a chump.

That was the first time I ever got dumped by a lady because I wasn't rough enough in the sack. Oh well, you win some and you lose some. I wished this had happened the first time we hooked up. I could've saved myself the guilt I was feeling for lacking the willpower to abstain.

*Onstage emceeing the show at The Ice House Comedy
Club in Pasadena, California in 2002.*

14

SOMEBODY'S WATCHING ME

La Jolla, California

The year was 1996, and I was living in San Diego, California. Michael Jordan quit his foray into baseball and returned to the Chicago Bulls. In 1996, the Bulls not only went on to accumulate the best record in the history of the NBA, but they won their fourth NBA championship. Seal was dominating the Grammys and the airwaves with his song "Kiss from a Rose."

I had been living in San Diego for over a year, trying to make the transition from Houston to Los Angeles. I had a brother, Edgar, living in San Diego, so I thought I could live in San Diego and commute back and forth to LA and do the Hollywood thing. One summer night, I was scheduled to perform at the Comedy Store in La Jolla, California. I really didn't want to be there because I was bored and ready for some action. Every so often I got the itch to go on the road and perform for hundreds of people. The crowd at the show on this night was light, so that made me less inclined to want to go up and perform. I kept thinking about leaving instead of doing a spot, but I grudgingly decided to stick it out and do a set. I had tried calling my friend Kristi, who lived right across the street from the Comedy Store, to come hang out with me, but she wasn't home. So I sat around brooding until I could go up and get my set over with. I was number five on the list of thirteen comedians.

My turn finally came and I went up to do my thing. There was a couple sitting all the way up front by themselves. Since I was in a foul mood, I gave them shit for doing so. While I chirped at them from the stage, I learned that they were tourists in town for a visit. San Diego is a beautiful sleepy town. Cool ocean breezes, luxurious hotels, and a laid-back vibe very different from the hectic ways of Los Angeles. San Diego seemed to be having the requisite effect on this couple. They came off as being exceedingly friendly and relaxed. The lady was very pretty with blonde hair and a nice, toned body. I could see that she spent considerable time in the gym. She reminded me of Loni Anderson from the old 1970s sitcom *WKRP in Cincinnati.*

When I finished my set, I got off the stage and headed for the pay phone in the lobby. I tried calling my friend Kristi again and this time she answered. As I tried to persuade Kristi to come and hang out, the blonde from the couple at the front table came into the lobby. She saw me and came over to introduce herself as Jennifer. Jennifer then told me that she thought I was funny, and she asked for my business card. I gave it to her, and then she said she had a question for me when she returned from the restroom.

The way Jennifer said "I have a question to ask you" piqued my curiosity. I told Kristi I was going to call her back and hung up the phone. When Jennifer exited the bathroom, she came right back over. She repeated her statement about having a question to ask me. Before Jennifer asked me the question, she said, "If you have a problem with what I'm about to ask you, I understand. I'll give you back your card and never bother you again."

Now my curiosity was really piqued, so I said to her, "I'm a comedian. What could you possibly ask that would embarrass me?" Then I said, "Go 'head and ask me."

Jennifer looked me dead in the eyes and said, "My husband wants to know if you would have sex with me while he watched?"

In my head, I was screaming, *What the hell! Are you serious? I can't wait to call Spence and tell him what this lady asked me!* But I didn't want Jennifer to see she had rattled me, so I played it cool and said, "Sure, I'm game." Then I asked, "Are you serious?"

She smiled and said, "Yes, my husband loves me, and I told him this was what I wanted to do."

I stared at her quietly for a few seconds, trying to figure out how this could be happening. Finally, I said, "Thirteen comics here tonight, why me?"

She whispered in a sexy, breathy voice, "Because you seem like a really cool guy." She then told me that she would be contacting me on Tuesday for our rendezvous.

I drove home immediately and woke up my buddy Markus "Markie" Holden. Markie was a funny comedian friend of mine from Houston who had moved to San Diego shortly after I moved out there. He didn't have any relatives in Cali, so he ended up renting out a room from my brother. I told Markie about Jennifer, how she looked, and her proposal. Markie's advice was plain and simple. He said, "I'd wear two condoms and bang her brains out." So much for rational advice from a friend and fellow comedian.

First thing Monday morning, I called my boy Spence in Houston and gave him the rundown on Jennifer. The thing I liked most about Spence, ever since we met in an acting class back at the University of Houston, was his sense of rationality. Spence was a cool brother who could look at any situation, remove the emotion, and look at it with a clear head. So after I told him about Jennifer's proposal, we considered all the angles as to why she and her husband would want me to do this.

At first we thought it was a setup, and they were probably trying to trap a brother and get me arrested for rape or something. But we quickly ruled that out. Then we thought maybe her husband was gay and that he really wanted to have sex with me, and this was just a ploy for them to get me to the room so they could tie me up and have him take advantage of me. When I told Spence that the husband was a neurosurgeon and she was a nurse back in Ohio, we kind of ruled that scenario out. The final theory we came up with was that Jennifer was a transsexual and I was being scammed. I told Spence that if Jennifer was a tranny, she was one sexy-looking tranny. The conversation lasted more than two hours. Finally Spence told me to get back to him with more details before I went over there, and we would try to nail down exactly what Jennifer and her husband were up to.

Tuesday rolled around, and like clockwork, Jennifer called me around noon. She introduced herself again and then asked me if I was still on board with the plan. I told her that I was still down. Then she proceeded to give me the layout of how things were going to go down. She said they were staying at the Hyatt Hotel in Mission Bay in the San Diego area and for me to come by around one in the afternoon. She and I would meet downstairs at the restaurant. We would order something to eat and then sit and chat for a while. Then her husband would come down and join us. When I felt comfortable, we would all go up to their room. Her husband would go hang out on the balcony, and she and I would get better acquainted in the room. She said that the door would be unlocked at all times, and I could leave at any time. She then asked me if I had any questions or reservations. I asked her again why she was doing this and if she was 100 percent sure her husband was down with the plan or if he was going to flip out when he saw me having sex with her. She told me not to worry and that this was something they had done before, so her husband was cool. She also said that she was a nympho, and her husband did whatever she wanted because he wanted to keep her happy.

I said, "Okay." I was about to hang up the phone when I thought of one more comment I had to make before I went over there. "Hey, Jennifer, one more thing: I am not into the gay thing, so make sure your husband knows this or we'll have a major problem."

She giggled and said, "I understand, and I assure you my husband is not gay either." With that said, I told her that we had a deal. She said, "See you at one o'clock" as she hung up the phone.

I immediately called Spence back and brought him up to speed. I told him that Jennifer was a nympho and just liked to get loose. Then I told him that they had done this before, so it wasn't like I was the first guy they were doing this with. I then told him that I gave her my "I am not gay speech" and asked her to tell her husband not to try any funny stuff. He said that if I felt good about it, I should do it. Then he told me to call and let him know how it went when I was done. After I hung up with Spence, I called Markie and told him where I was going to be; I even told him the room number and how long I was going to be there. I also told him Jennifer's name and that if I wasn't back by six o'clock, he should call the cops. He agreed, and I headed over to the Hyatt in Mission Bay.

On the drive over to the Hyatt, my heart was beating fast. The closer I got to the Hyatt, the faster my heart raced. I kept wondering what the heck I was getting myself into. Several times I thought about turning back, but I decided to go through with it because I was bored and slipping into a state of depression from lack of performing. There wasn't much happening in San Diego at the time, and that lonely, empty feeling was starting to come over me. I was ready for some adventure. Besides, something kept telling me that Jennifer and her husband were bluffing to see if I would really show up. I felt sure that at the last minute they would call and say they weren't really serious about the whole thing. I was determined to call their bluff and not let them punk me.

So I rolled into the guest parking lot at the Hyatt, and my heart was beating so fast that I had to sit in my ride for a few minutes and collect myself. I was pretty much hyperventilating. After I calmed myself down, I rang Jennifer's room and she met me at the restaurant downstairs. Jennifer came down in a short, sexy black dress and a pair of cute sandals. Her hands and feet were neatly manicured and painted bright red. She was sporting a pair of those huge Jackie O shades that made her look like a movie star. This woman was even more beautiful than I remembered from Sunday night.

Jennifer and I ordered a few rounds of drinks, and I launched into a series of questions. I pretty much asked her the same things I had before, such as "Why does your husband want to watch another man have sex with his wife?" "Are you sure he's down with this and there won't be any problems?" "Are you a man who's had a sex change?" I wanted to see her face and watch her responses when she answered. I figured that I could tell from her expressions if I was being set up or not. She gave me the same answers as before: her husband was cool with it and only wanted to please her. She laughed at the question about her being a man. She said there was only one way to find out if she was a man. Then she reached under the table, grabbed my hand, and placed it on her crotch. She wasn't wearing underwear, and again there was dew in the grass.

I gasped for air when I felt her wet coochie. I was so ready to jump between those thighs after feeling that, but I remained calm. I kept my hand there for a few more minutes, massaging her clit. I could tell she enjoyed my touch because she purred and told me not to stop. I was just starting to get into what I was doing to Jennifer under the table when a man suddenly joined us. I recognized him as the man who was with Jennifer at the Comedy Store the other night — and then I almost lost my lunch when Jennifer introduced him as her husband and he wanted to shake my hand. As I shook his hand and he sat down across from me and next to Jennifer, I felt funny. This was the first time I actually shook the hand of a man whose woman I was about to have sex with, and he was okay with that.

He ordered a drink, and we chatted about everything except what was about to happen between his wife and me. After an hour of small talk, Jennifer suggested that we go to the room. She asked me if I was still going through with the plan. I nodded, ordered one last shot of tequila, slammed it, and headed to the room with Jennifer and her husband.

When we got to the room, I was the last one to enter. As I walked inside, I immediately started looking around for any ropes, chains, or anything that could bind or knock me out. Jennifer's husband walked out to the balcony and lit up a cigarette. I kept my eyes on him because I wanted to make sure he wasn't going to try anything crazy with me. Jennifer assured me that the door would remain unlocked and that I could leave at will. There were two queen-sized beds in the room, and Jennifer sat on the bed closest to the door. Then she waved me over and pulled me down on top of her.

I kept swiveling my head back and forth, trying to keep one eye on Jennifer and the other on her husband smoking out on the balcony. She sensed that I was nervous and tried to put my mind at ease. She parted her legs and exposed her thick-lipped coochie. Then she put my hand on her crotch. My heart immediately started beating fast again. She reached for my crotch and started stroking me slowly. The more she worked, the faster my heart beat. Soon, we were out of our clothes, and next thing I knew, Jennifer and I were twisted up together belly to belly, smacking skin, which sounded like Fourth of July firecrackers. As I was doing Jennifer, I continued keeping one eye peeled on her husband. He was still standing on the balcony, smoking and sneaking peaks at what was happening in the room. I could bang his wife, but I could never be him. No way.

The first round happened faster than I wanted it to, but after I regrouped and got my second wind, it was on. Jennifer was very sensual and enjoyed every minute of our encounter. She bucked and clawed and talked dirty while we were throwing down in that room. I got so into it that I forgot about her husband. When we were done that second time, I was tired and hungry. Jennifer's husband asked if he could join us, but I lied and told them I had a show to do later that night, so I had to leave in order to get ready. By the time I had gotten dressed and ready to leave, Jennifer and her husband were going at it. They thanked me for coming by and told me to give them a call if I wanted to do it again. They said that they would be in town all week.

I hurried out of there and went straight home, where I phoned Spence and gave him the rundown. He was totally shocked that things went off with no problems. He said that I was living the California lifestyle now. I told him that I was thinking about going back for seconds on Thursday, and I would let him know how things went. I then looked for Markie and gave him the blow-by-blow details of my day at the Hyatt. He said that I should have spent the night.

Two days later, I went back for seconds. This time I stayed for three dynamite rounds. I wore Jennifer and myself out this time around. By the time I left she was sleeping soundly. Her husband had left after the second round. I wasn't sure where he went, but I thought I saw him down in the restaurant area when I was leaving. I never saw Jennifer and her husband again after that day.

Even though I enjoyed the excitement, I did beat myself up with mean thoughts followed by awful feelings for a long time afterward. I felt bad for not having the strength to say no and walk away from such a crazy proposition. I started wondering, *Was this the beginning of more wild sex parties? Where was it going to end?* I needed some help badly — I didn't want to end up another comedy tragedy before I got my "big break."

I began drinking more after that, trying to cope with my troubles. For a long time I went without any sex until I felt I had the monster within me under control. I withdrew from the people closest to me and started keeping to myself and even talking to myself. I was having a nervous meltdown, and there was nothing I could do about it. I started attending church and praying more, asking God to save me from my torment. Looking back now, I still don't know how I came through that period.

Onstage emceeing the show at The Ice House Comedy
Club in Pasadena, California in 2002.

15

LANGUAGE BARRIER

Hollywood, California

I finally moved to Los Angeles in the summer of 1996. When I first moved to LA and I was living by myself, I used to do temporary work to cover the bills in between comedy gigs. I got an assignment at one of the talent agencies, Writers & Artists. The place was a midsize agency with some big-name talent at the time. My assignment was supposed to last for a few weeks, so when I got there I kind of settled in. I was working in the mailroom with a bunch of twenty-somethings fresh out of college who wanted to be agents. These wannabe agents were called trainees.

I had worked in agency mailrooms before, so I knew the inner workings of the place. As a temp, one thing I learned was that if you wanted to survive on an assignment for any length of time, you had to stay out of the way of the regular employees. If they didn't like you for whatever reason, they would find a way to get you run out of that job. The mailroom was filled with a bunch of young, privileged white kids. The trainee in charge, John, was pretty friendly. I liked him. My assignment in the mailroom was basically working the fax machine.

It was my second day at Writers & Artists when I met Johnny. Johnny was a short Latin guy in his mid-thirties with an Afro. His dad was black, and his mother was from Santo Domingo in the Caribbean, so Johnny looked like a light-skinned brother, but he spoke Spanish fluently. I didn't know all this until a few days later. But the minute I met Johnny, I could tell he was from the streets. Johnny said any and everything that was on his mind, and every sentence ended with some kind of four-letter bad word. Johnny worked in the catering department. And he refused to pull any punches when he spoke. He was always giving one of the trainees crap about something. I could tell he intimidated some of them. Even though Johnny talked a lot of crap to most of the guys in the mailroom, he didn't do that with me. I guess because I kept to myself and he sensed that I didn't put up with that stuff.

Johnny quickly befriended me, probably because I was the only minority in the mailroom that he could relate to. When he found out I did stand-up comedy, he was always ragging on the trainees to hook me up with an agent or some work. One afternoon while Johnny and I were chatting, the cleaning lady came in to clean the wastebaskets, and I asked Johnny about her. He told me her name was Ana. Ana was in her mid-twenties, from Guatemala, and she didn't speak any English. She was finer than water in the desert and I wanted a sip.

Without asking me, Johnny started talking to Ana in Spanish. Up until this moment, I didn't know that Johnny spoke Spanish, but he did, and he did it very well. Johnny was also a practical joker, so he embellished what I said about Ana when he spoke to her. He told her that I thought she was cute and wanted to take her out. He said that I was going to be a big-time comedian so she'd better go out with me ASAP, sleep with me, and have a baby so that when I made it big, she could get a lot of money from me. Of course I found all this out later because I spoke not a word of Spanish. However, I knew he was telling her a good story from the way she was reacting and how he was laughing.

When Johnny was finished speaking to Ana, he told me what he had said. I immediately told her, "Do not believe him — he was lying!" I don't know if she understood what I said, but she smiled and nodded.

Then Ana said something to Johnny, and I asked him what she'd said. He said she wanted to know my name and whether I was working there now. Johnny told her my name was Jeff and that I was going to be working there for a few weeks. He also told her that I was good in bed and she should go out with me. That was Johnny, always causing mischief for laughs at someone else's expense.

Ana left, and Johnny and I continued talking about her. He said that if he weren't married he would make a move on Ana himself. I agreed with him because even though Ana was wearing the typical cleaning-woman smock over a pair of pants, I could still see that she had a nice body. She was about five feet five inches with long black hair, and she didn't wear makeup outside of some lip-gloss. I remember thinking to myself that I definitely wouldn't mind hooking up with Ana, but I knew it wasn't going to happen because she didn't speak English and I didn't speak Spanish.

As the days went by, Ana would always wave at me whenever she saw me around the agency. If she came into the mailroom and none of the trainees were around, she would attempt to speak to me. I would always have to tell her to wait and summon Johnny to be my interpreter. Over the next few days and weeks, I learned quite a bit about Ana. She had been living in Los Angeles for over five years but had never learned to speak English. She lived with her parents and other siblings in a three-bedroom apartment in Hollywood. Because Ana was in America illegally, she had never ventured out at night for fear of being caught and deported back to Guatemala.

Even though Ana didn't speak English, she appeared interested in getting to know me. Just when I was starting to get used to working at Writers & Artists Agency, I was told my assignment was ending. I told Johnny that my last day was that Friday, and he said he would try to set something up with Ana for me. All the time I was working at Writers

& Artists, Johnny always talked about coming out to see me perform. At the time, I was a regular performer at the Ice House Comedy Club every weekend. I told him to set up a date for him, his wife, and Ana to come and check me out in action. He spoke to Ana and his wife, and everything was in motion for the upcoming weekend that Saturday night. The show was at 8:00 p.m., so the plan called for me to pick up Ana while Johnny and his wife would meet us there. Johnny was going to serve as my interpreter throughout the night of our double date. Johnny got Ana's address and gave it to me. I was supposed to call Johnny before I left my place to go pick up Ana, and he was going to call her and let her know I was on my way.

That Saturday I had to get up and teach a comedy traffic school class, so I was up early and was gone all day. When I got home around five, I tried calling Johnny with no success. I jumped in the shower and then tried calling him again, but I still wasn't able to reach him. For the next hour I tried in vain to reach Johnny. I kept getting his answering machine. It was time for me to leave to pick up Ana, and I still couldn't get in touch with Johnny. At first I thought about just forgetting the whole thing and going to the show by myself. Then I thought how Johnny had told me Ana was looking forward to finally going out. I also thought about how she'd been living here in Los Angeles for over five years but had never been out anywhere. It was then that I made the decision to pick up Ana and take her to the show. However, before I did that I ran out to the bookstore to pick up an English-to-Spanish dictionary.

As I drove to Ana's place, I tried to figure out how the heck I was going to communicate with her. Nervous, I pulled up in front of Ana's apartment building and noticed it was a secured building, which meant I was going to have to get buzzed in before I could get up to Ana's apartment. I used the intercom and buzzed Ana's apartment. Someone answered in Spanish. I asked for Ana, but the person on the other end apparently didn't speak English, so they hung up on me. Now I had to figure out how to get into the building. I decided to wait until someone exited the building to walk in. As I was waiting for a resident of the building to walk in or out, I looked at my watch and saw that I was running out of time. It was almost show time at the Ice House Comedy Club, and I had to get there fast. I was emceeing the show and couldn't afford to be late.

Within five minutes, someone walked out, so I snuck in and sprinted up the three flights of stairs to Ana's apartment. As I ran up the stairs, I hoped that Ana answered the door when I knocked because I was getting the feeling that no one in Ana's family spoke English. I found Ana's apartment, and as I knocked on the door, it opened. I peered in, hoping to see Ana, but no one was in the living room. As I was standing there knocking and looking into the apartment, an older woman came to the door. I started flipping through my dictionary, trying to find the right words to ask for Ana. Just as I was about to say something, Ana walked into the living room as though she was going to the kitchen or to some other room in the apartment. When I saw Ana, I yelled out her name, and she looked over at the door and saw me. She immediately grabbed her purse and her jacket, and we were off to the Ice House Comedy Club.

As I sped up the 110 Freeway to Pasadena, I tried to engage Ana in conversation. First I complimented her on her appearance. Basically I was speaking American Spanish — you know, where you add the letter *o* after certain words. For example, when I told Ana she looked real sexy in her jeans, top, and heels, I said, "You look nice-o a noches."

Ana asked me something about Johnny's whereabouts. At least I guessed that's what she was asking me because she said something with Johnny's name in the sentence. I couldn't look in my English-to-Spanish dictionary while I was driving, so I just kept speaking American Spanish: "Senor Johnny no come-o. He got sicko." I guess she understood because she smiled and nodded. Then she sat back and started listening to the music that was playing on my car stereo. I was playing my 2Pac *All Eyes on Me* CD. I could tell she was enjoying it because she started nodding her head to the beat.

We got to the club just as the show was about to start. When I walked in with Ana, I saw a few of the male comedians checking her out. I sat Ana in the back on the right side of the showroom. Then I asked her if she wanted anything to eat. I looked in my dictionary and I saw that the word for eat was *comer*. Just in case I was saying the word incorrectly, I also asked her using American Spanish, "Do you want some food-o?" To really drive the point home, I used my hands in an eating gesture just so she would know what I was talking about. I'm not sure if Ana understood me, but she smiled and nodded. I started to ask her what she wanted to eat, but I figured that would take another ten minutes, so I just went ahead and ordered her some wings and fries. I figured everyone liked wings and fries. If not, I would eat it. I also ordered Ana a Corona so she could wash down her dinner.

As I went onstage and did my thing, I noticed Ana laughing. I wasn't sure if she was getting the jokes, but she looked as though she was enjoying herself, so it was all-good to me. Every time I got offstage, I would go over by Ana's table and check to see how she was doing. I kept looking in my English-Spanish dictionary for the right words, but it wasn't working, so I just started giving her the thumbs-up sign. She just kept nodding her head in the affirmative. She had eaten most of her food and drunk a couple Coronas, so I ordered another round of drinks for her. The show ended around ten thirty. I grabbed Ana and we hit the road. I kept trying to ask Ana if she wanted to go anywhere else. Since I couldn't understand what she was trying to tell me, I decided to take Ana home and then call it a night.

When I pulled up in front of Ana's place, I told her in the best American Spanish that I could think of how much I enjoyed her company. "Ana, I had a good-o time-o. Hope you did to." Then I got out and walked around to open Ana's door so that I could escort her to the front door of her building. When I opened her door, she just sat there like she didn't want to move. Then she motioned with her hand for me to come close to her. I thought she wanted to kiss me, so I leaned in, but she pulled back. Then she motioned with her hand for me to sit next to her. So I closed her door and walked back to the driver's seat. As I was walking back, I wondered what she could possibly want. I actually hoped she wanted to mess around, but I had already told myself that I wouldn't try anything with Ana since we really couldn't understand each other, and I didn't want any misunderstanding between us. I sat back down in my seat and closed my door.

There was an awkward moment of silence that seemed to last for hours, but soon, Ana started talking. However, she was speaking so fast that all I could get out of the conversation was that she wanted something from me. I told her that I didn't understand what she was saying by shaking my head back and forth and saying, "No understand-o." I guess she got it, because she started making a gesture with her hand as though she was talking on the phone. So I asked her if she wanted my number. She shook her head as if to say yes while she said, "Sí, sí." I gave her one of my business cards. She looked at it, saw my picture, and gave me a big hug and a kiss on the lips before she jumped out of the car.

I had to hurry to catch up with her. By the time I caught up to her, she was already going inside the front entrance to her building. I walked her up to her apartment, and when we got to the front door, she put her arms around me and gave me the deepest French kiss I could want. We hung in kiss mode for a while before she finally went inside.

As I headed up the 101 Freeway to my place in Hollywood, my mind replayed the last few minutes with Ana. I thought about how excited she got when I gave her my phone number. I started wondering if she'd been trying to ask me for my number all night but I just hadn't understood her. Just as I pulled into my parking space, a crazy thought entered my mind. How was Ana going to call me on the phone and speak to me when neither one of us could understand each other? By the time I got to my apartment on the fourth floor, I figured she just wanted it as a keepsake to show it off to her girlfriends. I opened my front door, went inside, changed my clothes, jumped in my bed, and didn't think anything else about it.

I always sleep in on Sunday mornings, but this particular Sunday after my date with Ana, my phone woke me up real early. It was eight o'clock, so I wasn't a happy camper when I answered the phone. It was Johnny calling. The first thing he asked me was, "Did you hit it last night?"

For a minute, I didn't know what he was talking about, and then I caught on that he was talking about Ana. I told him, "No! I was on my best behavior." He started telling me how Ana liked me a lot, and that I could've slept with her if I had really tried. I let Johnny know that was not my intention for the night. I was only trying to show Ana a good time, and that was it.

Then I asked him why he hadn't shown up or called to let me know he wasn't coming. He said his wife had an allergic reaction to something she ate, so he rushed her to the emergency room, and they pretty much stayed there all night waiting to see a doctor. Thankfully his wife was doing better now. We talked for a few minutes on the phone, and he said he would talk to Ana and call me back later and tell me what she said. I hung up the phone and went back to sleep.

Johnny called me later that afternoon to tell me that he'd spoken to Ana. He said she thought I was a nice gentleman on our date. Since my assignment had ended, I wasn't going to see Ana at work anymore, so Johnny said he would keep me updated on what Ana was thinking.

I really didn't expect to hear from Ana again, but a week later she called me out of the blue. I was so surprised when I answered the phone. All I heard on the other end was "Jefe, Jefe, Jefe." At first I thought she had the wrong number and I was about to hang up. Then I recognized Ana's voice.

I said, "Hey, Ana, how you doing?" Then I caught myself and repeated the little bit of Spanish I knew. "Ana, cómo estás?" I guess she thought I'd learned Spanish within the week since we last saw each other, and she just started rattling off a whole conversation. I had to tell her to hold up. Then I put her on hold and dialed Johnny on the three-way phone line. I was in luck because Johnny answered the phone, and I quickly brought him up to speed on what was going on. I then clicked over and he started talking to Ana. Then he would translate to me what she was saying. Basically, Ana wanted to know how I was doing and when she could see me again. We made plans to see each other the following weekend when Johnny was available.

Ana would call me a few more times after that, but we never went out again because I could never line up her and my schedule with Johnny's. Every time she called me, I would call Johnny on the phone. Sometimes I got him and sometimes I didn't. I moved to a new apartment shortly after I met Ana, and my number changed. Since I never had Ana's number, I didn't have any way of getting in touch with her. She had stopped working at the agency, so Johnny had no way of contacting her either. That was basically the end of my short romance with Ana. Our language barrier turned out to be too wide a chasm to overcome. To this day, I wonder if she ever got her papers so she could stay in America legally, if she became a naturalized citizen, or if she ever learned how to speak English. Wherever she is, I hope she's doing well. She was a really nice lady.

The thing I was most proud of about that situation with Ana was that I was able to overcome the inner voices of torment and not succumb to my shortcomings with females. Even though I wasn't dating anyone at the time, I was able to stick to my game plan and not sleep with Ana just for the heck of it to stave off my sexual cravings. Perhaps the language barrier had something to do with it, or maybe it didn't. The bottom line was I didn't sleep with her, despite how much I wanted to, so I took my small victory and moved on.

Onstage emceeing the show at The Ice House Comedy
Club in Pasadena, California in 2002.

16
POLE POSITION

Canoga Park, California

It was the spring of 1999, and I was finally starting to adjust to living in LA. This was the year we saw President Clinton nearly get impeached by Congress for having an affair with Monica Lewinsky. It was also the year that Lauryn Hill's album, *The Miseducation of Lauryn Hill*, won a Grammy for album of the year. A lot of sisters used to be jamming that album after it went to number one on the charts. Jackie was no different.

I met Jackie while driving down Western Avenue in Hollywood, California, on a Sunday night. It was like a real-life version of that old 1980s arcade game Pole Position, where you would get behind a pseudo steering wheel and race simulated drivers. I was returning home from visiting a former coworker of mine. I noticed this car kept speeding off from the light at the intersection every time it would turn from red to green. The funny thing was, every time the motorist would speed off, I would see them at the next intersection. Traffic was light that evening, so I would always pull even with them when I got to the intersection. After this happened a couple of times, I decided to look and see who was driving the car. To my surprise, it was an attractive caramel-colored sister with a pretty smile. I am such a sucker for a pretty face and a nice smile.

When I looked at her, she waved at me, and I waved back. Just then the light turned green and she took off speeding again. I was for sure I wouldn't see her again after that. To my surprise, she got caught at the next red light, and again we ended up right next to each other again at the intersection. I looked at her and shook my head. Then I rolled down my window and asked her, "What's your name?"

She replied, "Jackie!" I then motioned for her to pull over. She shouted back, "Nope, you could be an axe murderer!"

I told her I left my axe at home so she was safe and it was okay for her to pull over. She laughed and took off. This time I took off behind her and told her to pull over. I promised her that I wasn't an axe murderer. She asked where I wanted her to pull over. I told her, "Anywhere you feel safe." She then pulled over into the parking lot of a busy Asian grocery store. I pulled up next to her, and we got out, leaving our cars idling.

To my surprise, she was wearing a pair of shorts and a cashmere sweater. She was a little shorter than me. The thing I noticed most about her was that she had some nice, thick thighs (just the way I like them) and two gigantic breasts. I'm not much of a breast man, but I was already fantasizing about laying my head down on those two watermelons she had sitting on her chest. I introduced myself and asked her if she always pulled over for strangers on the side of the road. She said, "Only on Sunday nights and when they swear to me that they're no axe murderer."

I could tell that she had a sense of humor, and I liked that in a lady. I asked her where she was speeding too. She said she was on her way home, so I gave her my card and told her to give me a call when she got home. She then wrote her number down on a piece of a paper and gave it to me. She said she would be home in thirty minutes, and I could call if I wanted to; then she jumped back in her car and proceeded to speed home.

I was living in Hollywood, California, at the time, so I was less than five minutes from my place. When I got back to the crib, I told my buddy Spence about Jackie and how I met her while driving down Western a few minutes ago. Spence had just moved to Los Angeles and was sleeping on my couch until we could upgrade to a two-bedroom apartment. He was intrigued by how I was able to pull a beautiful lady while driving down the road. I told him that it wasn't the first time it had happened. Since moving to Cali, I had been pulled over several times by women while driving on the freeway or surface streets. The first time it happened, I was a little scared because I was on my way to San Diego, and it was two girls trying to get me to pull over. I thought they were up to something, but I figured I could take both of them if they tried anything, so I ended up pulling over and chatting with them for a few minutes. They lived in Oceanside and wanted me to come party with them anytime I was going to be in the area. I told Spence if he lived in Cali long enough, he would experience the same thing too.

I called Jackie an hour after our impromptu meeting. I wasn't dating anyone at the time, so we chatted for several hours getting to know each other. I learned that she was three years younger than me. She was also a single mom who had just moved out to the Valley because of her job. She had her own place and worked right around the corner for a big health insurance company. We talked every night for a week and finally made plans to go out on our first date. It was a Thursday lunch date. I'd noticed that some women made sure their first date with a guy was during the day. That kept a man off balance because he didn't know if the date was just a friendly thing or something more. At lunch, a lady had to get back to work or return to running her errands. At night there wasn't usually the same dynamic. She was free, and that freedom would force her to make a decision about how much she liked me and when or where the night would end.

So I knew Jackie was feeling me out by keeping our date to a lunch, and that was cool with me. We went to a Chinese restaurant close to her job. The date went well, and I dropped her back off at work when we were done. That evening while we were talking on the phone, she invited me over to her place for dinner the following Saturday night.

She lived in a two-bedroom apartment on the second floor, and it was nicely furnished. It was easy to tell that an adult lived there. She had candles lit, and we sat down to eat with jazz playing on the stereo. When we finished with our meal, we moved to the couch and continued our conversation over several glasses of merlot. I hate merlot because it's dry. I like my wine like I like my ladies — sweet. I drank the merlot because I thought I would score points with Jackie. As we drank, I got looser and friskier. Before I knew it, we were deep into her California King bed. I ended up spending the night. Jackie sure knew what she was doing in bed. She was the type of lady who expressed herself with sex. It wasn't just a series of acts for her, like it was for some women, but an extension of her fun-loving personality. I was hooked worse than a fish.

For the next few months, Jackie and I were inseparable. We did a lot together those next few weeks. We went to a jazz festival, the movies, out to dinner, bowling, and on short weekend getaways to Santa Barbara, Las Vegas, San Diego, and Corpus Christi, Texas … We were having a lot of fun and just as much sex. And we were doing the dirty everywhere too. One time during the middle of the day, we had sex right there on the hot beach sand in Santa Barbara. Jackie sat on me and placed a towel on top of her so it looked like we were just hugging and kissing each other. It was a weekday when most people were at work, so there weren't a lot of people around. The few stragglers who were around were too busy doing their own thing to notice us. If they did, nobody said anything.

Another time, Jackie and I had sex in the women's restroom at a comedy club I had just finished performing in. We hung around drinking, chatting, and singing karaoke with the staff. At 1:30 a.m., the manager locked the club doors, and we kept on drinking and partying. At some point I went to the bathroom to take a leak. When I was done, on my way out of the men's restroom, I saw Jackie going into the women's restroom. So I followed her in and then inside the stall. Next thing you know, we're in the stall doing it doggy style. We were going at it for a few minutes when we heard someone walk in. I looked through the crack of the stall and saw that it was one of the female staff members we were just singing with. I guess she heard the ruckus we were making when she walked in because she bent down and looked under the stall we were in. Then she went into the stall next to us. Now why the hell would she do that? We stopped what we were doing until she was finished.

I guess there was no toilet paper in her stall because she asked us to pass her a roll. There was a roll loose on top of the toilet in our stall, so I tossed it over to her. I guess she wasn't expecting it to come to her that way because it fell on the floor and rolled right back over into our stall. She started giggling and said, "Can you send it again?" This time Jackie did it the normal way, passing it under the stall hand to hand. The girl finished her business and left the restroom. Before she left, she said, "I'm leaving now so you all can finish." Then she started laughing and exited. Jackie and I got back at it as soon as we heard the door close. When we were done, I exited quickly, hurried into the men's restroom, and cleaned myself up. That was a fun night.

Jackie and I were getting along pretty well. For a while I was starting to really feel like she was my girlfriend. Like any relationship, we had our ups and downs. We would occasionally argue about living together. As much as I liked Jackie and liked hanging out with her, I wasn't ready to live with someone just then. One night I took her to my show at the Ice House Comedy Club in Pasadena. She said she liked my set, but I could tell something was bugging her. I found out what was bothering her the next weekend, when we got into our first big fight.

The next weekend I didn't have anything to do, so I decided to chill at her place and catch a couple basketball games on television.

When I told Jackie about my plan, she got extremely pissed off. She just didn't understand how I could just sit on the couch and do nothing. The argument escalated to the point where she told me to get the hell out of her place. I was shocked. Before I left she told me that I needed to change my comedy act onstage because at times it looked like I was flirting with some of the women in the audience. There it was! The truth. The thing we were really arguing about. I packed the few items I kept at her place and left.

That was the beginning of the end for Jackie and me. We ended up having an on-again, off-again relationship for the next few years. We would get together from time to time whenever neither one of us was dating someone. That was cool with me because I needed my space to continue pursuing my dreams. However, the more I hung around Jackie, the more I saw how controlling and bossy she was. She was always trying to tell me what to do. If there's one thing I hate, it's when someone I'm dating constantly tries to boss me around. Whenever she would start trying to boss me around, I would pack my stuff up and hit the door. Other times I would stop calling Jackie for several weeks. Jackie had grown on me a lot, and I really missed her when we weren't together, but I just couldn't be with someone who was so controlling and had insecurity issues that caused conflict between us.

When I met Jackie, I told her about my problem as a sex addict. I wasn't going on the road as much, so she suggested I seek therapy. It was during this time that I started seeing a therapist extensively for my problem. I bounced around to a few different therapists before I found a female therapist whom I felt comfortable enough with to start being honest about my feelings. She told me my issues were very common, and it would take time for me to overcome them. While dating Jackie, I started feeling better about controlling my addiction. Too bad Jackie and I didn't make it because I was starting to fall for her.

*Onstage emceeing the show at The Ice House Comedy
Club in Pasadena, California in 2002.*

17

THREE HOTS AND A COT

Sherman Oaks, California

The year 2000… the new millennium, was upon us and I was on my way back home to St. Thomas for the first time in twelve years. The Los Angeles Lakers had just defeated the Indiana Pacers for their first NBA championship since Magic Johnson retired. Shaq and Kobe had finally arrived on the world stage. This was also right around the time the entire cast of the hit sitcom *Friends* signed a two-year contract paying each actor $750,000 an episode. I made a mental note to remember this so I could tell my mom when I went home. I figured she would cut me a little more slack as a comedian if she saw what my future earning potential could be.

I met Linda on the dance floor at a club called the Mill in St. Thomas, US Virgin Islands. I really didn't think anyone outside my family would remember me nor did I expect to have much fun since I didn't know anyone — at least that was what I thought. I was pleasantly surprised. All my siblings had returned home for the summer, and even though I didn't graduate from high school in the Islands, I still had a lot of friends there. My siblings knew all the hot spots to hang out in. Earlier in the week, I ran into an old girlfriend that I'd dated before I left the Islands twenty years earlier. We had lost contact over the years. I told her I was staying by my parents, and she promised to call and make plans to get together before I left. At the time, I was feeling confident about my relationship issues. It had been a while since I'd had that lonely, empty feeling and the yearning for any kind of connection. It seemed the therapy was working, so all I had to do was stay with it and keep the faith that things would continue to get better for me with my love life. I just had to stay focused and fight the urges whenever they started creeping in.

I pretty much hung out at my parents' house all week. The weekend rolled around, and I was itching to go do something. My brothers told me the lime that night was at a club called the Mill up in the hills on St. Thomas. ("Lime" is Island slang for "hangout.") I'd been away from the Islands for so long that I really didn't know where the Mill was, but my siblings assured me I would like it there.

Saturday night came, and I got ready to roll up to the club around ten. My brothers looked at me like I was crazy. I'd forgotten I was in the Islands, where the clubs don't start until late. Ten in the evening was early. My brothers started teasing me, calling me a Yankee (Island slang for someone who moved to the United States and had forgotten his Island culture.) So we sat around killing time till we were ready to go to the club. I opened a bottle of Cruzan Rum, coconut flavor, and we started drinking and reminiscing about the good old days when we were growing up in the Islands.

By the time I was buzzed, my brother and my cousin were ready to roll up to the club. We rolled up to the club, paid the cover charge, and went inside. It was around eleven thirty, and the music was bumping. There were a few people at the club, but it wasn't packed. I walked onto the dance floor, where several women were just shaking and swaying to the music. I thought to myself, *I'm going to have a ball in this club.* So I was feeling like the man when I strolled up to the first sexy lady I saw and asked her to dance. She replied, "No!" I went over to the second sexy woman dancing up a storm on the floor, and she said, "Nope!" The third lady I asked also said no. For a minute I stood there wondering why women came to the club to dance by themselves. These women were pretty much having sex with themselves on the dance floor, grinding and holding hands. I said to hell with it — I liked to dance, and I refused to let a few women stop me. I went on the dance floor and started dancing by myself. One hour went by and I was still out on the dance floor shaking my ass.

The DJ was jamming dancehall, reggae, and hip-hop, and I was feeling it. By the second hour, the dance floor was packed. I was sweating and grooving to the music when I noticed that several women had moved into my personal space to dance with me. I really didn't care because I was enjoying myself, and the ladies were sexy and knew how to shake it. By the start of the third hour, I was dancing with a cute little fine-ass honey with a short Halle Barry hairstyle. She and I were really getting caught up in the sexy atmosphere. For the next three hours, we worked up a sweat dancing exclusively with each other. At the end of the night, I thanked her for the many dances and walked away. I found my cousin Terence "TC" Hodge, and we started to bounce. TC was one of my younger cousins who practically grew up with my siblings and me. He was muscular with a quiet demeanor. TC asked me if I got the girl's number. I said, "No."

He asked, "Why not?"

I said, "Why should I? We were just dancing."

TC just looked at me, shaking his head. "Because she liked you. Couldn't you tell?" To be honest, I really didn't think about it. I liked to dance, so I was just out there doing what I liked to do. Then I stopped and thought about what TC said and went looking for my dance partner. I found her by the exit talking and laughing with a few guys. I walked up to her, told her my name, and asked her for her number. She told me her name and told me to give her my number. I gave her one of my comedy cards with my nationwide pager number on it, and she said she would call the next day.

The next day my entire family went to Tortola, British Virgin

Islands, to visit. While I was over there, I got a page from my dance partner. When I checked it, the voice mail read Linda. She said she was just calling to say hi and to make sure I had given her the right number. When I got back to St. Thomas, I called Linda and we set up a lunch date for the next day. Because I had been gone for so long and didn't know where I was going, my cousin TC had to drive me to Linda's job to get her. TC dropped us off at a real nice Island restaurant close to her job in Frenchtown. I instructed him to come get us in an hour. We went into the restaurant, and Linda ordered the fish and I ordered the oxtail meal. Over lunch I learned that Linda was valedictorian of her high school class. She was thirteen years younger than me and had been at her current job for several years. She asked me if I was really a comedian. Like most women, she thought my profession was interesting. I liked Linda's personality. She was funny in a dry, offbeat kind of way. We then made plans to go out later that night after she got off from work.

Again, because I didn't know my way around the Island, I took another cousin of mine, Daphne, to find Linda's house. She lived on the eastern part of the Island, out in the country. It took a while but we found it. After I picked up Linda, we dropped my cousin home. Then Linda and I went to a sports bar and shot some pool. I learned that night that Linda was a purebred pool shark. She was knocking them down like Minnesota Fats. I lost a few twenties that night. After she lightened my pocket, we drove to the Marriott Hotel by Frenchman's Reef and hung out for a while, sipping on drinks. When we were done, I dropped Linda off and went home to my parents' house and fell asleep in the living room in front of the television.

I didn't see Linda again until the following Saturday night. We made plans to see each other that weekend at the Mill. I got there around eleven. There were a lot of people at the club, but my cousin TC saw Linda while he was walking around and let me know. Linda and I went on the dance floor and didn't get off until the club closed down five hours later. I learned something else about Linda that night: she knew how to drive but didn't have a license or a car. I agreed to take her home. My brothers had also come to the club that night in another car, so TC rode home with them while I took Linda home that night.

On the drive to her place, Linda informed me that she didn't allow men to come to her house. I was the first guy that she was allowing to see where she lived. I asked her why she was bestowing me with such an honor. She said that because I didn't live on the Island, she figured she didn't have to worry about me stalking her. When we got to Linda's house, we sat outside in the car talking for a minute. Linda told me that she would invite me up, but her place was a mess. She asked me to give her a few minutes and said she'd call me when she was ready.

Ten minutes after she went upstairs, Linda stood out on the porch and called out for me to come up. I had to walk up a series of stairs to get to her place. When I got inside, Linda was standing there with a sheepish look on her face. The place looked pretty clean to me. Later on I would learn that her place was usually a filthy mess with clothes thrown everywhere. Apparently when she went upstairs, Linda picked up everything—clothes, dirty dishes, toys, etc.—and tossed them all into the closet.

We sat around making small talk, and next thing I knew, Linda and I were sexing each other crazy. Linda was good in bed. I really enjoyed having sex with her, and I ended up spending the night.

I woke up early the next morning because I had to get the car home before seven, when my parents had to go to work. Before I left Linda's place, I made sure I hit it one more time just in case this was destined to be a one-night stand. I left when I was done and sped home like a guilty teenager to make curfew. I was trying to get home before my parents woke up, but I was too late. My mother was already in the kitchen making breakfast. As I walked in, she gave me that look as if to ask, *Where are you coming from this time of morning?* I knew my mom. I knew she wanted to ask me but she never did.

I had a week left on the Islands, so Linda and I hung out again that following Wednesday night. Another thing I liked about Linda was that from time to time she would wear different wigs, and it would change her appearance and make her look that much cuter. We went out for drinks, and at the end of the night we ended up making out in my car. Linda was definitely a good piece of tail. The upcoming Saturday was going to be my last, so again we made plans to meet at the Mill.

When Saturday night rolled around, my cousin TC and my brother, Jah Weeble, went to the club around ten thirty. When we got there, we thought the place was closed because there was no one in the club. The place looked deserted. The doorman assured us that it was going to be packed and we just got there too early. We decided to go sit out in the car and kill some time. While sitting out there, we drank a bottle of Cruzan Rum, pineapple flavor, straight from the bottle. By the time we went back in the club around eleven thirty, the place was packed and I was buzzed. This was my last night on "the Rock," so I planned to make the best of it. (Rock City was another name most Islanders called St. Thomas.)

On the way in, I saw Linda playing pool on the other side. She saw me as I strolled over to the dance floor area. I was standing there trying to watch the people dance, but the place was spinning. Well, what do you know, I was drunk. This was the first time I'd ever been drunk in my life, and I was doing everything in my powers to stay vertical, but it was tough. Just then, Linda showed up, and we danced the night away. I don't know how I did it, but I never fell out (at least that's the way I remembered the night). I'm not sure what I looked like dancing that night, but Linda never complained. I must've sweated some of that alcohol out of my system because when it was time to leave I drove Linda home. When we got to her place, we ended up having sex four times that night. Linda was insatiable—she loved sex. I had to put some extra work in when she and I did the horizontal dance. I must have blown out three or four discs in my back wearing her out.

I was leaving on Monday, so I spoke to Linda the day before. She said that she had never been to Cali and was thinking about using her vacation to come visit me. I told her that she could stay with me when she hit town. We exchanged contact information, and I left to go back to Los Angeles first thing that Monday morning. Linda and I stayed in touch over the next few months, and she did come to visit that September. I took her to all the tourist spots in Los Angeles and she had fun. We got down and dirty every day and night too. I started thinking, *I could get used to this kind of sex every day.*

Linda went back to St. Thomas. We talked on the phone every week and e-mailed each other every day. Once a week, I would send her forget-me-nots via mail. She liked when I did that. One day while talking to Linda on the phone, she informed me that she was contemplating leaving St. Thomas to finish college. She said she could either go to New York, where she had a sister, or she could come to Los Angeles. I told her that if she wanted to, she could move to Los Angeles for college and stay with me. Without missing a beat, she said, "I'm moving to Los Angeles."

Right before Linda moved to LA, I started to feel as though I had made a big mistake. I had everything to lose and she had everything to gain. I wanted to call the move off, but it was too late. Linda had already quit her job and given up her apartment. Linda and I ended up living together for three years, but it was a rocky three years. The minute she arrived, I immediately felt the stress of her moving to Los Angeles. Aside from the thirteen-year age difference between us, Linda didn't have a driver's license, a job, or any friends. Getting Linda up to speed with a new job and her driver's license took an emotional toll on me.

Even though Linda knew how to drive, she didn't know how to drive on the big highways here in America. I had to sign her up to take a driving class. Then I signed her up with a temp agency, where I had a friend working. She was able to secure a job working at a big bank in downtown Los Angeles. I found out after Linda moved to Los Angeles that she wasn't the most outgoing person. She was friendly but she was too shy, so making friends was not her strong suit. Because she didn't have any friends or family in Los Angeles, all of my free time was spent with her. This really started to wear on me because I soon learned that Linda and I didn't have a lot in common. The thirteen-year age difference was also creating a problem. When I had a problem and needed someone to talk to, all she could do was listen. She couldn't really give me any rational advice or support. The sex was still great, but mentally, it was wearing me down. While I was trying to get Linda straight, I started turning to my previous girlfriend, Jackie, for comfort. This was a terrible idea, and I knew it at the time, but Jackie was the only person I could think to confide in. Yeah, I had a lot of male friends, but sometimes a man needs a woman's ear and counsel.

The three years Linda and I lived together, I went through so much emotionally that there were times I wanted to strangle her. The three things that created the most friction in our relationship were financial problems, cleanliness, and baby-daddy drama. I really dug Linda. In the beginning I really thought she could be the one. I wanted us to get married and have a baby together. The more time went by, I realized that I was really putting myself way out there on a limb and digging a financial hole with her. I helped Linda move to the mainland. I'm not sure if it was because she was so young, but I noticed that she was easily influenced by what guys said to her. I was constantly worrying about some other guy coming along and stealing her away after all the effort I put in getting her set up in Los Angeles.

Like I said, when I met Linda, she was twenty-one years old, and I was in my mid-thirties. Linda was a nympho in bed, but she was also a slob and exceptionally bad with money. She had a bad habit of bouncing checks all over the place. She just didn't understand the concept of not writing checks if you didn't have money in your account. After not heeding my warnings about writing bad checks, she was finally contacted by the Los Angeles District Attorney's office. They threatened to put her in jail if she didn't take a check-bouncing class and made good on a couple of her outstanding checks. I had never heard of such a thing as a check-bouncing class, but apparently it existed for first-time offenders. She had to spend a Saturday in a class with a bunch of other check forgers. I guess it was safe to assume she didn't pay for the class with a check.

We also argued about her baby daddy. Linda had a four-year-old daughter named Christine, who eventually came to live with us the second year we lived together. Christine was a sweet little girl, but Linda would always get into it with her baby daddy, who still lived back in St. Thomas but was trying to regulate how we should raise Christine. I didn't have a problem with him having an input in her upbringing, but he wasn't paying any child support, and he would call all the time trying to give Linda instructions on how she should do things for Christine. Yeah, right — I wasn't having any of that. If he wanted to have a say in how she was being raised, he needed to bring his ass to Los Angeles and take Christine to live with him. Until then, he needed to stay his ass in St. Thomas and let us do what we had to do. Linda didn't agree with this, and there was always tension in our relationship because of it.

And it didn't help that she was a slob. I can't tell you how many times I came home and the dishes were piled out of the sink, the garbage was overflowing, and there were clothes thrown everywhere. Linda's answer to this pigpen was, "Let's have sex." Don't get me wrong, I stayed horny and would've liked nothing more than to bend her over until I couldn't cum anymore, but I suffer from obsessive-compulsive disorder. Whenever I came home and the place was filthy and Linda wanted to have sex, the brain in my head wouldn't allow me to follow the brain in my pants. Instead of boning, I would start cleaning up. There was nothing like coming home for a quickie and getting stabbed in the butt by a fork that was buried under the blanket on the couch.

On a few occasions when the place was messy and Linda wanted to have sex, I remembered saying to her, "There is more to life than sex." Never in my lifetime had I ever thought I would use that phrase on someone that I was dating. Not me, Mr. Sex Addict, the guy who loved sex as much as he liked breathing. Many times I wished I had met Linda back in my twenties when sex was my number-one priority. Don't get me wrong, I still liked sex a lot, but now in my thirties my priorities had changed somewhat. I was getting older, so I needed to reevaluate my purpose in life. Sex was still in the top five things I wanted, but it wasn't first on the list anymore.

I wanted to leave Linda so badly, but I felt bad for her. I couldn't just walk out on her because she came thousands of miles to be with me and it wasn't working out. She didn't have any other family or friends in Los Angeles, so I felt obligated to take care of her. Besides, I really cared about her, and deep down I still wanted our dysfunctional relationship to work. Many times Linda would tell me she wanted a boyfriend, not a father. Essentially, that was what I had become to Linda: a father figure looking out for her and her daughter.

Jackie knew my situation with Linda and how unhappy I was, so everything between us was up front. We started hanging again whenever I wanted to get away from the stress at home. I was naïve thinking I could be friends with Jackie. Spending time with her was a big mistake because she had other plans. I guess she still liked me and wanted me back, but this never occurred to me until it was too late.

One day after I left Jackie's place and went home, Jackie followed me twenty minutes later. She had never met Linda, so that day she was intent on doing so. I don't know how she got through the front door because my building was supposed to be secured; I guess she followed behind someone as they walked in. I had just settled into my room to talk with Linda when I heard this loud knocking and screaming at the apartment door. "Jeff, come out here! Come out here now!" At first I thought I was dreaming because this kind of thing never happened to me before. Then I looked through the peephole and saw that Jackie was really standing there yelling and screaming for me to open the door. Linda was so scared she ran into the bathroom and called my boy, Big Fran. While she was on the phone explaining the drama that was unfolding at our front door, I was in the living room trying to figure out how to deal with Jackie. I was going to ignore her, but she was yelling so loud. I knew she was disturbing my neighbors and embarrassing the heck out of me.

So I decided to step outside to try and calm her down. As soon as I cracked the door, Jackie bum-rushed inside, knocking me back, and we crashed to the floor. She immediately tried to get up and run in the bedroom where she thought Linda was hiding. I grabbed her in a bear hug, and she flayed her arms wildly, punching and kicking me. We crashed into the dining room table and knocked it over. There was a vase on the floor, and next thing I knew, she slammed the vase into my forehead. I almost passed out, but I knew if I did Jackie would catch up to Linda, and then there wouldn't be any telling what would happen. I started to use brute strength to get control of Jackie and managed to push her out the front door and close it. During our struggle, Jackie's keys had fallen out of her pocket. She started pounding on the door telling me to give her the keys so she could leave. I refused to risk opening the front door again. She was damn near frothing at the mouth, and I didn't want a repeat of our slapstick routine. I told her the cops were on their way and she was going to jail. I was so furious at that point; I wanted to see her ass get locked up. With all the commotion going on I was sure that one of my neighbors or Linda called the police.

Sure enough the LAPD showed up and put Jackie, Linda, and me in handcuffs until they sorted out what was going on. Because Jackie didn't live there, she was taken into custody. My heart broke seeing Jackie hauled off by the cops in handcuffs. I never thought I would picture her getting served three hots and a cot. But through that incident with Jackie, I finally got what I'd been hoping for: an end to my relationship with Linda.

Linda was so traumatized from this incident she decided to look for her own place and moved out. Before she moved out, she started sleeping with a butter knife under her pillow. One evening I asked her what she planned to do with the butter knife —butter her attacker to death and clog up his arteries? It was my attempt at humor and trying to make light of a bad situation. She didn't get it. She just looked at me crazy and made me promise not to remove her knife when she was sleeping. Eventually Linda and I went our separate ways, and she moved to the East Coast.

Posing with a few childhood friends after performing at Jay's Place 2 in Stone Mountain, Georgia in 2011 (left to right: Lauren "Ren" Gumbs, Jeff Hodge, Derek "Makim" Hodge, and Jeffrey Hughes Sr.).

18
THE ONE

Covina, California

I met Renee while I was working Street Team Promotions for 94.7 the WAVE, the jazz radio station in Los Angeles. It was a part-time job I took more for the events than the money. We would probably work once a month from March to September, the time of year when there were all these jazz festivals in Southern California. There's nothing like going to one of those events and seeing so many beautiful women. It was a guy's heaven just to be able to walk around and mingle. Because I worked for the WAVE, I was in a very good spot: the WAVE booth. We used to sign people up to win a free trip anywhere around the world. As the people came to sign up, I would chat up the ladies. Because we were always giving away something free, sometimes the women would stick around and chat with me for a minute, trying to get free stuff, such as CDs, T-shirts, coffee mugs, concert tickets, etc. On top of all that, because the WAVE was a big radio station here in Los Angeles, we were usually one of the sponsors for the jazz festivals.

Sometimes at some of those events, the WAVE would have a private booth to entertain some of their big clients. Whenever the WAVE had a booth, we got to eat and drink for free. I used to joke with my buddies and tell them the WAVE paid me to eat, drink alcohol, and mingle with good-looking women; from my point of view, the only thing better than working for the WAVE was doing stand-up comedy.

So I was working at the Pasadena Jazz Festival located in the parking lot of the Rose Bowl. It was the last day of the event and I was inside the WAVE booth, just sitting around chatting up the listeners and encouraging them to sign up to win a trip anywhere in the world. As I was doing this, I noticed a very short, sexy lady with the prettiest smile I'd ever seen walking up to the booth with her friend. They asked what freebies we were giving away. That was my opening, so I told them they could get whatever they wanted. I introduced myself and asked them if they had signed up to win the trip anywhere around the world. Tonya, who was the more outspoken of the two ladies, said no, so I gave her the pitch and she signed up. While Tonya was signing up, I turned to her friend and asked her name. She smiled and said Renee. I told Renee that she should sign up too, and she said she would. Then I asked her where she'd go if she won the trip. She replied, "Sydney, Australia." I thought it was a good choice, considering that was one of the places I wanted to visit myself. When Tonya finished, she gave the book to Renee to sign up.

As Renee was signing up, I started chatting up Tonya. She was friendlier than Renee. I would later find out why that was so. Tonya wanted some free stuff, so I went into my personal stash of good stuff to give away and gave them some swag. I learned early when I started working for 94.7 the WAVE that it was best to go through all the free merchandise and pick out what you wanted and stash it away, because by the time the evening was over, there wouldn't be any of the good stuff left for you. I gave Tonya and Renee some WAVE water bottles, CDs, and decals. I also told them that I was a comedian and they should come and check out my next show. I gave them both my business card and asked where they were going from there. Tonya said they were getting ready to go home because they had been there all day. They said good-bye and walked away.

As they walked away, I immediately went to the sign-up sheet for the trip giveaway, looked up their names, and copied their information. The information requested on the sign-up sheet was their name, mailing address, phone number, and e-mail address. Tonya filled in everything, but I noticed that Renee had only given her name and e-mail address. I wrote down both Tonya's and Renee's info for later use. I wasn't sure what I was going to do with it, but I figured I had to figure out a way to see Renee again.

Since Linda and I broke up, I had moved out from our apartment in North Hollywood and went to stay by some relatives in Hawthorne. I pretty much just slept there because I was gone most of the time. I was working for a law firm in Santa Monica while I finished getting my bachelor's degree that summer. I figured I would stay by my relatives until I graduated in the next few months, and then I would get my own place at the end of the summer. One night when I got home from my law firm gig, I was messing around on my computer and decided to take a chance and send Renee an e-mail. The e-mail was brief. It pretty much said, "Hi Renee, this is Jeff, the guy from the WAVE booth at the Pasadena Jazz Festival on Sunday. Just wanted to say that it was nice meeting you and hope to see you at my show one of these days in the near future." When I sent that e-mail to Renee, I didn't really expect to hear back from her. My mom would always say to us, "Closed mouths don't get fed."

A week went by before I got a response from Renee. To be honest, I had already forgotten that I sent her an e-mail, so when I saw her name in my inbox, I was surprised. Her response was, "Hi Jeff, nice meeting you too. I am curious to know how you got my information?" I immediately responded that I had pulled it off the win-a-trip sign-up sheet, and if she didn't want me contacting her any longer, I wouldn't. I knew pulling her name off the sheet was against company policy, and I could lose my job for doing so, but I figured I'd take the chance anyway. The worst that could happen was either she wouldn't respond or I would get a nasty e-mail from her telling me not to contact her anymore. I could live with either of those scenarios.

A few more days went by, and she replied saying that it was cool, she just wanted to know. I told her that if she wanted to we could talk on the phone, but she said communicating via e-mail was good enough for her for the time being. So for the next several months Renee and I wrote each other via e-mail. In the beginning, I did most of the communicating, trying to find out what made her tick. She usually responded to my e-mails several days after I sent them. I was cool with that because it wasn't like I had anything going on. Besides, I was still trying to get Linda out of my system. Even though we didn't make it, I still cared about her a lot. I constantly worried about her and her daughter. I hoped they were doing fine.

As time went by, Renee started opening up to me more. I remember telling her that my graduation from California State University, Northridge was coming up, and she wished me congratulations. She said that perhaps we could go out and grab a drink sometime and celebrate. That sounded promising to me, and I told her to let me know when she wanted to go. Her response time to my e-mails went from several days to daily.

While we were communicating via e-mail, I learned a lot about Renee. I learned that she was five years older than me. She had been married for twenty-five years. The last five years, she had been going through a divorce, but her husband was contesting it bitterly. She had two kids, a boy and a girl. Her daughter was attending college, and her son was a senior in high school. She was an elementary school teacher, and she was a very private and cautious person due to a few prior bad experiences with men.

Renee gave me her phone number shortly after that, and we talked every day. July rolled around, and Renee and I set up our first date. We initially met at a Starbucks Coffee in Pasadena and talked for hours on end. She was a huge baseball fan and loved to dance. The Los Angeles

Angels was her favorite team. Our first date went well. Our next date was a few weeks later, and we went dancing. Because she loved to dance as much as me, we went to one of my favorite dance clubs in Pasadena. It had three dance floors: hip-hop, house, and R & B music. The crowd was younger, twentyish, but it didn't matter. We had fun. All night I kept testing Renee by trying to get really close up on her, but she wasn't having none of that. Her not letting me do that told me that I still had some work to do before she would sleep with me. That was cool with me since I wasn't planning on going anywhere. I was really starting to like Renee. She was a classy lady and I was hypnotized by her style. She had me doing things I didn't ordinarily do.

Renee was an avid bike rider, so we would meet early some Saturday mornings and go ride the trails. One of our favorite bike trails was off the 605 Freeway in Cerritos. Sometimes we rode all the way down to Long Beach. I came to learn that Long Beach was Renee's favorite city in Southern California. Sometimes after we got down to Long Beach, we would park and lock our bikes and then eat lunch or hang out on the waterfront. Occasionally afterward, we would meet later that evening and go out. Renee and I were definitely getting closer to each other.

One day during the early fall, Renee asked me if I wanted to attend a function with her on Saturday night. I told her sure, and she gave me the information and mentioned that it was formal. She had finally let her guard down enough to tell me to pick her up at her house. I was blown away because I had gotten to the point where I had given up on her ever inviting me over to her place. Like that old saying goes, "When you least expect it, that's when it happens."

That Saturday, I had to teach a traffic school class out in the Inland Empire area all day. Since it was closer to Renee's house, I told her that I would come straight from my class and change my clothes there. When I was done with my class, I called Renee, and she gave me the directions. Because this was before navigational systems, I had to look it up in my Thomas Guide map book. She lived in a gated community in Covina. When I went inside, Renee introduced me to her son. He was a nice kid, and I spoke to him for a few minutes. I took a bath in her downstairs bathroom, got dressed, and then we headed out. The function was at the Old Mining Factory Restaurant off Interstate 10 in Pomona. Renee and I looked good together as a couple. We had a good time that evening eating, drinking, dancing, and chatting with her friends.

When we got back to her place, Renee told me that I could spend the night if I wanted to, but I would have to sleep in the guest bedroom downstairs since her son was home. That was cool with me. She went upstairs to her room and changed into her pajamas. I changed into the clothes I was going to sleep in (T-shirt and shorts), and we met in the den to watch television. Her son was watching TV upstairs in his room while we were downstairs. At first we really were watching television, and then I decided to push the envelope and see if I could get lucky. I initially started massaging her neck and then I worked my way down to her lower back. Since she was lying on her stomach, I then started caressing her legs and rubbing her feet. I could see that she was becoming more relaxed, so I repeated this entire process one more time.

As I was massaging her back, I switched tactics and started massaging her inner thighs with one hand. I noticed that as I did this, she didn't try to stop me, so I continued massaging her neck and rubbing her inner thighs. Before long, I noticed her legs started spreading wider. When I saw this, I slowly started working my one hand up her inner thigh toward her fuzzy triangle. When I got there, I gently touched it and pulled back a minute to see what her reaction would be. She let out a gentle moan. A moan meant that I had a green light to proceed. It was go time. I massaged her clit slowly, and I could feel her getting hot. The more I did this, the more she purred and let out moans of pleasure. By this time, I was caressing her breasts with my other hand. I could tell she was really getting turned on. I did this for a while, and then she just stopped me cold and told me she had to go check on her son.

She ran upstairs. I heard her open a door, say something, and then she ran back downstairs. She lay back down on her back and said, "You can continue." I didn't waste no time — I dove in her lap and performed oral sex on her. By the time she was having an orgasm, I had already pulled off all her clothes. I was so hard and ready that by the time I got all my clothes off, it was on. As excited as I was, I took my time making love to her that night because I knew if I did it right the first time, she would come back for more. We both climaxed around the same time. That was a wrap for the rest of the night. I knew we'd be an item after that.

Renee and I were inseparable after that weekend. We primarily saw each other on the weekends because we both worked and lived so far away from each other. I was living in Hawthorne and she lived in Covina, which was forty-five minutes away without traffic. I did stay over by her a few times during the week, but it would take me almost three hours to get from her place to my job in Santa Monica in the morning. The old saying about traffic being a bitch in Los Angeles really is true.

For the next year Renee and I were together, we did so much. She was the type of lady who enjoyed getting out and doing things. We went everywhere and did everything together. She wasn't like most forty-something women I had dated before. She loved sex a lot, which was cool with me. Most of our evenings ended with us messing around. We officially became a couple that November. I remember us going to a Christmas concert sponsored by the WAVE with some of the biggest jazz performers in the world. The concert was in Long Beach, and we had such a great time that to this day, every time I hear one of Norman Brown's songs, I can't help but think of Renee.

That same fall I had a college gig to do up in Northern California at California State University, Monterey. Renee rode up there with me for the gig. We drove up there that Friday, checked in, I did the gig, and then we hung out for the rest of the weekend. It was cold as an ice tray that weekend. I remember because Renee didn't like the cold, and I kept stopping on the wharf to check out the scenery. She would just keep on walking. My brother used to live in Monterey back in the mid-1980s, and I went to visit him a few times, so I vaguely knew my way around. They had a comedy club there in Monterey, and before I went up north, I called and set up a showcase. The club management told me to come in Saturday. I went in for the first show, and they put me up after the emcee. I had a good set. The owner promised to book me, but nothing ever came of it. That's the nature of the comedy business. Nobody really wants to book you until you have a name or good management. Once you have one of the two or both, then the comedy club bookers fall over themselves trying to book you into their venues.

On the drive back to Los Angeles, Renee and I took the scenic route, the 101 Highway. It was a longer drive but we weren't in any hurry. We got to see the coast and all that came with it. I love barbecue, so we stopped at a barbecue restaurant along the way. I don't recall the name of the restaurant but it was good. We kept passing vehicles parked along certain spots on the coast. I remember saying to Renee, "I wonder what they're doing?"

She said, "It's obvious they're having sex." Up until she said that, it didn't occur to me that was what they were doing. I thought the drivers just pulled over to rest their eyes from highway fatigue. Not to be outdone by them, I found a space somewhere along the 101 Highway, backed in our vehicle, and parked. We were in Renee's Jeep, so we had plenty of room inside. We climbed into the back and got to playing with each other. There was nothing like having an orgasm and hearing the ocean waves crashing against the rocks below. I wished we could stay in that moment forever, but we had to get back to the grind of everyday life. Later on the journey, Renee confessed to me that our little rendezvous along the roadside was the first time she had an orgasm in a car. I didn't know how to take that, but I was glad I was able to please her, if only for that one day.

Later that year, around Thanksgiving Day, I met Renee's mother. She lived down in the San Diego area, so we drove down there and had dinner with her a few days before Thanksgiving Day. Her mother seemed like a nice lady. Every time I met one of Renee's people, I felt as though I was being evaluated as a potential mate for her. Stuff like that never really bothered me because I had been through it before with my daughter's mother's family, and I learned how to put it out of my mind. I had come to realize that people will like or hate you regardless of what you do.

I spent that Christmas with Renee. She and her kids were there at the house. Throughout the day, other family and relatives stopped by and celebrated with us. This was the first Christmas that I had enjoyed in a long while. Renee and I exchanged gifts. That same holiday season, we went with some of her friends to see George Lopez in concert for New Year's Eve at the Gibson Amphitheater at Universal City. I had a great time and so did Renee. Matter of fact, I always had a great time when I was with Renee. I had really fallen for her and it was getting scary. I was starting to get into that area of the relationship where I had no control over my feelings and was vulnerable to someone else's whims. What if she wanted to break things off? I would be helpless. I usually put up walls to keep from getting to this point in a relationship. I'd been hurt a few times and didn't want to go through that intense pain again. I would rather die before I felt that helpless, brokenhearted feeling again. I started wondering if I should pull back, but things between us were going too well. I thought I had finally found the one.

The following summer, Renee and I went on a seven-day cruise to the Caribbean. It was an African American cruise. I had never been on a cruise before, so I was really looking forward to going with Renee. I really thought our relationship was taking off because within a year of meeting Renee, here we were on the open seas cruising with each other. Renee had planned the cruise before she met me. Initially, she was supposed to be going on the cruise with some of her girlfriends, but they all flaked out on her, so when she asked me, I said yes. I didn't know what to expect, but I did plan for us to have plenty of fun. We flew from Los Angeles to Puerto Rico and boarded the ship there. It was on Carnival Cruise Lines, one of their fun ships. I noticed when we got on the cruise there were more women than men on board—a two-to-one or maybe even a four-to-one ratio. Yes, indeed, there were a lot of pretty chocolate women on that cruise. Despite that, Renee and I spent most of our time on the cruise together.

However, the few times we weren't together, watch out. I remember that on the first leg of the cruise from Puerto Rico to St. Thomas, I was walking around trying to find my way back to our room from the casino and I ended up on the elevator with a beautiful woman. She was almost not human; she was so gorgeous—she was more like a creature than a person. We started talking, and she asked me if I was on the cruise by myself. I told her that I was cruising with my girlfriend. Without missing a beat, she pulled out her business card, wrote her cabin number on the back of it, and said in the sexiest voice she could, "I'm in cabin 229. Feel free to come by and get anything you want." Then she handed me the card. Before she walked off, she leaned in real close and whispered into my ear, "When I say anything, I mean *anything!*" She stuck her tongue in my ear and walked out of that elevator swishing her hips.

My heart was beating so fast I told myself I needed to get my ass back to my cabin before I got myself into some serious trouble. That lady had gassed me up so much that when I got back to our cabin, I was horny. Renee and I had a quickie before we ventured out to check out the ship together. I never told Renee about that incident, but for the rest of that cruise I stopped looking at women altogether. Whenever a lady looked in my direction and smiled at me, I would look at the floor and shuffle away. That was how I knew I really had fallen for Renee. I didn't want to risk cheating on her, getting caught, and losing her. I remember thinking that I was deep in love, and I hoped it turned out good in the end.

For the most part Renee and I got along fine; at least that's what I thought. We never got into any arguments, and we always did a lot together. I looked forward to the weekends and spending time with her. Looking back now, there were a few things that should have caused me concern. Many times when we were together, Renee would point out how other couples interacted with each other. She was always comparing their PDA (public display of affection) to ours. I remember holding Renee's hands, hugging her, and even kissing her in public. But no matter what I did, I guess it wasn't enough or I didn't do it the way she wanted me to.

I remember a couple of incidents in particular. One time she even counted how long I held her hand. The second incident was when she had her daughter check us out when we were out on a double date with her and her boyfriend. Her daughter said we looked more like friends than a couple. I agree that I was never the most affectionate guy in public. I was never a huggy-huggy, kissy-kissy kind of person. I believed in doing other things to show her I cared, such as giving her "Thinking about You" cards or sending flowers to her job or house. I figured she would appreciate these gestures and cherish them enough to ride out the rough times in our relationship. I figured wrong.

The next thing that should have raised a red flag with me was the amount of attention Renee got. Renee got so much attention from other men that one would swear she was Halle Berry. The constant attention didn't bother me because I knew Renee. She wasn't one to just go out with men because of who they were or what they had. What bothered me were the exes who wouldn't let her go when it was over. Her estranged husband was still trying to get back with her. Then there was the previous boyfriend before me who used to call, e-mail, and text her every day. He used to reach out to her, begging her to take him back all the freaking time. I can understand when a person you love breaks up with you and you're trying to win them back, but when it's been over six months, it's time to let them go and move on. I used to ask Renee why she would even entertain those guys. The estranged husband I could understand. She had to talk to him because they had kids together, but I would tell her to keep it strictly business and to disengage when he veered to other topics such as "we" or "us." The ex-boyfriend was a nutcase. He would call or show up at her house and drop gifts off for her all the time. I tried telling her how every time she took his call or answered one of his e-mails, she was giving him hope, but she thought that if she was nice to him, he would go away quietly. That never happened. He was still there creating havoc when Renee and I broke up a year later.

Speaking of breaking up, yes, eventually Renee and I broke up. I still remember the day she called me and told me to meet her at a Starbucks in my neighborhood. I was so naïve about what was about to go down that I showed up bearing gifts from a recent three-week comedy tour I did in the Middle East. When Renee told me she wanted to leave me, it hit me like a sledgehammer. I could barely breathe. I asked her why. She said we didn't have any chemistry. I never took chemistry in school, but I knew chemistry and we had it. I asked her to give us time to work it out, but she wasn't having any of that. She had already made her mind up. To add insult to injury, she had me meet her in a public place to break up with me. I guess she thought I would act a fool like some of her exes did when she broke up with them. That was not my style. When you tell me it's over, I may cry and try to plead my case, but I wouldn't act a fool. The way she did it hurt me just as much as the actual breakup itself.

I remember driving away from that Starbucks and calling my friend Beth in San Diego to tell her how Renee had just dumped me. I went home, crawled in my bed, and cried myself to sleep. When I woke up I called my inner circle of friends (Spence, Big Fran, and my brother Jah Weeble) and told them what had happened. I told them how I felt like jumping off a bridge to ease the pain. I was a basket case for the next few months. I would go to work, come straight home, and crawl into bed. I didn't go anywhere or see anybody. At least my buddies always said the right things to make me feel better for the moment.

One of the things I remember them saying that kept me from hurting myself was this: "Go ahead and kill yourself, but long after you're gone, she'll be here fucking someone else!" That sobered me up. I never thought about killing myself after that. I didn't want her to win. In addition, something my mother told me back when I was growing up helped me to get past the pain and anger of that broken relationship. My mom would always say to us when we were growing up, "Every disappointment was for a good. You may not see it today, but somewhere down the road you will, and you will thank the Lord." I have used those words many times over the past decade to comfort me in times of sorrow.

I never believed in that saying "the one that got away." However, with Renee, I would definitely have to say that she was the one that got away. It took me a long time to get over her, but eventually I did.

Inside a Black Hawk helicopter on our way to entertain the troops at Bagram Military Base in Afghanistan in 2005.

19

You Can't Handle the Truth!

Manas Air Force Base, Kyrgyzstan

I was sitting at home recuperating from knee surgery when my phone rang. It was a male voice on the other end of the phone asking me if I wanted to go to the Middle East to entertain the troops. This was something I'd always wanted to do, but I'd never gotten the opportunity to do so. I was kind of out of it because I was under the influence of Vicodin, so I vaguely remembered telling him I would do it. I gave him my e-mail, and he promised to send me all the information I needed.

It took two months for us to get all the necessary paperwork, medical shots, and military clearances completed. Now here we were, on November 1, at the home of the booker, going over the last-minute details about the tour. I didn't know the other three comics I was going with. Chris Moser was a Caucasian comic who acted like he knew everything. He was a nice guy, but he could be freaking annoying at times. No matter what the time or place, he was always doing parts of his act whenever you had a conversation with him. Barry, the booker, made Chris the de facto road manager for the tour. Just from Chris's attitude alone, I could tell we were going to clash on the tour. Warren Durso was a short, pudgy, outspoken Caucasian comic from the East Coast. He was a chain smoker but he was a cool dude. Matter of fact, he was so cool I gave him the nickname "Warren G" after the West

Coast rapper from the LA area. Although Warren G was the oldest of all four of us comics, he was the practical joker of the group. Richard "RV" Villa was a cool Latin comic with a medium body frame. He was the youngest of the bunch and pretty much got along with everyone on the tour. He also had game when it came to the ladies.

I had never done a USO tour before so I was nervous. I was even more nervous when I learned that we might have to go to Iraq to do some shows because the war was really raging over there at the time. Barry the booker assured us that we would be safe over in the Middle East for the three weeks we would be there because we would have the world's most powerful military protecting us. Go USA! That surely calmed my fears. Then he gave us a check for half of our pay, answered all the questions we had, and gave us back our passports and our itinerary. (We had to submit our passport to the Pentagon to get military clearance to get on the bases.) We were scheduled to perform in eight countries for the next three weeks. The first stop on our itinerary was Kyrgyzstan. I had never heard of the place before, but I was game for the adventure.

It was a twenty-plus-hour flight from Los Angeles to Kyrgyzstan. We made two stops along the way. We flew from Los Angeles to Chicago. Then we flew on to London's Heathrow Airport. We had a couple hours' layover there in London, but I didn't chance a try with the local delicacy: fish and chips. I had heard mixed reviews from friends who had visited England, and the review always ended with a long trip to the bathroom. From London, we flew to Kyrgyzstan. When we arrived it was late and cold as an icebox. I remember I kept thinking to myself this was supposed to be the Middle East—what happened to the 120-degree temperatures? The airport almost seemed abandoned. I don't know if it was because we got in so late or because Kyrgyzstan was not on too many tourists' lists of places to see.

After we cleared customs, two male personnel from the US Air Force greeted us. My knee was hurting from the long flight and I was starving. The two military attachés were very personable. One of our military chaperones was John. He was tall and very friendly and also very talkative. The other military chaperone was named Patrick. He was about my height and also very polite. We learned that they would be our liaisons for the two days we would be staying at Manas Air Base there in Kyrgyzstan.

The first day we spent getting familiar with the base. It was a big, sprawling place with lots of military personnel and equipment. Our liaisons came and got us first thing that morning and took us to get breakfast. Breakfast was buffet style and all you can eat. The food was great. It was like eating in a diner back in the States. Everything was fresh and fluffy and savory. I really didn't want to leave the buffet, but after an hour or so we were taken to meet the commanders of the base and ailing troops in the hospital. Apparently when you performed on those USO tours, they attached a photographer with each group on every base, so our photographer was busy snapping pictures of me and the other comedians wherever we went.

We took pictures with all the troops we saw, and the word started getting around that we were the comedians. Buzz built around the base that we had arrived and were scheduled to perform later that evening. While visiting the gym on the base later that afternoon, I ran into a couple of female air force cadets. The ratio of men to women on the base was something like fifty to one, so whenever I ran into females, I made it a point to speak to them. I quickly exchanged introductions with these female soldiers. Jenny was the hot, petite Filipina in her early twenties while Stefanie was the hot Caucasian chick in her early twenties with the sassy mouth. I asked them if they were coming to the show later on that evening. Stefanie replied, "Only if you're funny!" Then they both started laughing. As they got up to leave, Jenny promised me that they would come to the show and bring some of their other female friends along.

I was pumped up. I went back to the comedians' sleeping quarters, which was a very large tent in the male section of the base. As cold as it was, we had a heating unit in our tent that kept it warm. That warmth made me think of my new friends. I told the other comedians that I ran into some hotties on the base and invited them to the show. Needless to say, they were pleased by that revelation.

Showtime was set for 8:00 p.m. When I got to the showroom my mouth dropped. The place was packed with over five hundred air force and military personnel. I ran into Jenny and Stefanie at the makeshift bar. They had brought along two more hotties just like they'd promised to do. Stefanie introduced us. Nicole was the petite black chick in her mid-twenties with the soft, sexy voice and Halle Berry hairstyle. The other new friend was named Sharon. She was Caucasian in her early twenties, with more of a rugged shape than her friends but still cute. Nicole and Sharon asked me if I was funny and said that if I wasn't they could boo me with no regrets. Then they all started cackling as they walked away to their seats.

I ended up closing the show that night and had a really good set. When I came off the stage, I walked over by the ladies. They loved my performance and started asking me a bunch of questions. I got something to drink and bought all the ladies a round. As we stood there conversing, Nicole moved to come stand right next to me. Because it was loud inside the showroom and she was shorter than me, she kept pulling my head down to her mouth so she could whisper questions in my ear. When she found out that I lived in LA, she wanted me to give a kiss to some director friend she went to school with who lived in LA and was working for MTV. I told her I wasn't going to kiss a guy. She said she would give me the kiss, and I could deliver it any way I wanted to. Of course she told me all that before she told me she was married. Then she asked me if I was married.

Jenny, the Filipina, bought me a drink and asked me to dance. She was a girl fighting in a war half a country away from her homeland, but she was full of joy, and let me tell you, she could move her thang. While

I was dancing with Jenny, she informed me that she was married, but her husband was stationed back home in the States. Then she pulled my ear down to her mouth and whispered, "What my husband doesn't see happen, he doesn't have to know about."

Just then the song ended and Nicole and Stefanie walked up. Nicole handed me a drink and pulled me close to her. I definitely sensed that Nicole was getting flirtier as the night went on. However, she kept talking about her husband, so I figured she wasn't just married but happily so. I excused myself to go to the bathroom.

Since it was a temporary base, all of the facilities were a short distance away from the showroom, which gave Chris his chance. When I returned from the restrooms, Chris was there holding court with Nicole and the girls, doing his act for them again. As I walked up, Nicole came over to me and held my hand. Just then, Stefanie leaned over and whispered something in my ear that caught my attention. She said, "I have some of the best coochie on this base. You better get it while it's hot!" Those words alone had me hard instantly. Nicole saw Stefanie whispering in my ear and pulled me away from her. What Stefanie said intrigued me, but I didn't understand why Nicole was acting the way she was. One minute she was acting like she liked me. Then the next minute she was talking about her husband. However, the minute her two friends started flirting with me, she began acting jealous.

Chris told me that we had to do an impromptu mini show later on for the Eighty-Second Airborne Battalion that missed the show because they were getting ready to be deployed downrange. He gave me the details for the impromptu show and then left me on my own. I guessed he somehow knew I would have my pick of the ladies. No man worth his testosterone wants to play off the bench. If he can't be the star on one court, he moves on to a game that he can win. Chris was going to plant his flag elsewhere. But I could have used a wingman just then. Too bad my cousin Claddy didn't make the trip with me.

Nicole said she wanted a copy of my book, but I didn't have any on me. I informed her that all the copies were back in the performers' tent. She said she would walk over there with me. Military rules did not allow male and female soldiers to congregate in the sleeping quarters. I guess because I wasn't in the military, Nicole totally ignored this rule, came right in, and laid herself across my cot. Then she started cooing about being cold and that I should come warm her up. Up until that time, I had no idea what this lady was up to. I have to admit that it was very cold that night. I think the temperatures were hovering in the twenties.

I lay down beside Nicole, and the minute my body hit the cot, she was all over me kissing and groping. At first her actions took me by surprise because I thought she was happily married, but then my instincts kicked in, and the next thing I knew, we were tearing off each other's clothes and getting into a frantic boning session. As we were going at it, I thought to myself, *Wow, is this how the entire three weeks in the sand is going to be?* After we finished, I quickly got dressed because I had that impromptu show to do. We snuck out of the tent and headed over to the show location. I went up and did a quick fifteen-minute set. When I got offstage, Nicole was out of sight, gone, nowhere to be seen. At first I thought she was in the bathroom, but after ten minutes she wasn't back, so I went looking for her. I ran into Nicole's girls and asked them if they had seen her. They all said no. For the next hour I walked around that base looking for Nicole with no success. I eventually gave up, returned to my tent, and called it a night.

The next morning we got up early, ate breakfast, and then flew out to our next destination. The next base we went to was in Qatar. After we landed, we went and did some meet and greets with the top brass and the troops. Then we went and ate lunch. After lunch we were on our own until show time later that night. I decided to go to the computer center and e-mailed Nicole. I asked her where she'd disappeared to the previous night and then ended the e-mail by telling her that I hoped that she was all right. I signed off and went to catch a nap. I woke up to the other comedians getting ready to go eat, and I quickly got ready and joined them. I soon learned that the show wasn't happening until the next night, so after I ate I went back to the computer center.

When I logged on I noticed that I had an e-mail from Nicole. I opened it with much anticipation only to be shocked by the contents:

> *Hello, Mr. Hodge. Glad to hear that you made it safely to your next destination. I'm going to cut to the chase and ask you one question. Did we mess around last night? If so, that was not my intention. The only person I'd planned to have sex with was my husband. I was drunk last night, so I was not aware of anything that may or may not have happened between us. When I disappeared, I went to the bathroom to throw up. I got so sick that I went to my bed after I left the bathroom thirty minutes later. Please let me know because I would like to get to the bottom of this matter. Thank you.*

This e-mail not only shocked me but scared the crap out of me. My second day on the tour and I was about to catch a rape charge. WTF! My mind was racing. The events of the previous night with Nicole replayed in my mind. Nicole never looked drunk to me. I bought her one drink, and I saw her nurse that drink for pretty much the rest of the night. She was the one who initiated the contact between us after the show and in the bed. She never once told me to stop when we were getting down. Matter of fact, she insisted that we do it again when we were done. I was the one who had to tell her to stop because I had another show to do. I used to work at a law firm, so I knew that I had to be careful about what I said in my e-mail reply to Nicole, or it could come back to bite me in the ass. My response to Nicole, via e-mail, was this:

> *Nicole, I am glad to hear that you're doing well. As far as last night's events, nothing happened between you and me that you*

didn't want to happen. Everything we did was consensual. Besides, I didn't know you were drunk because I only saw you drink one beer the entire night. You looked and sounded fine to me when you were in my company. We seem to have a difference of opinion on what transpired last night. Perhaps you will rethink your position after this e-mail. Take care.

I was sweating bullets after I received that first e-mail response from Nicole. My mind was a complete wreck. I didn't know what the heck to do or who to talk to. I kept envisioning myself getting arrested on the tour and thrown in jail in Qatar. I figured since I was a US citizen, touring abroad on US military bases as a civilian, the military would probably have to send me back to the United States for a trial. Damn, how was I going to face my mother and tell her about this? I didn't have any appetite for the rest of the evening. I just moped around. I kept going back to the computer center every couple of hours, checking to see if Nicole had responded. No such luck. I figured I would have to sweat this out until I heard back from her. And then who knew what the hell she would say next? Until then, I would try to go about my usual daily routine.

The next day I tried to lie in my cot as long as I could. When I finally got up, the other comedians had already gone and eaten breakfast, so I grabbed some breakfast by myself. We had some meet and greets to do with injured soldiers after we finished with breakfast. When we got to the hospital, all the soldiers, injured and non-injured, were glad to meet us. We shook hands, told jokes, and took pictures with pretty much everyone in the building. I really enjoyed meeting the troops and visiting with them, and I let them know this. I eagerly thanked the soldiers for their sacrifices out there on the battlefield. Without them, I couldn't totally be me, travelling and entertaining people. I made sure I thanked each and every one of them whenever I got the opportunity to do so.

The meet and greet took up several hours and helped to take my mind off of the problem that was brewing back in Kyrgyzstan. It was already dinnertime, so I decided that I would check my e-mail after I ate. That dinner was the longest meal of my life. Not that I ate much, because I didn't. I pretty much sat around the dinner table playing with my food, listening to the other comedians joke around. After I finished not eating, I rushed over to the computer center and jumped on the first open computer. The minute I logged on, I noticed that I had an e-mail waiting for me from Nicole. I felt my heart stop as I clicked on the link. Man, I couldn't even breathe. This was Nicole's response:

> *Mr. Hodge, if we had sex the other night then you took advantage of me when I was drunk. My husband was the only person I ever planned to have sex with. However, I am not trying to get you in trouble nor ruin your career, so I will keep this between us. Please do not contact me after today. Good luck with your career and the rest of the tour.*

All I could say after I read that e-mail was, "Damn, I dodged a freaking bullet! Now I knew how those celebrity actors and professional athletes felt when some of these women come out of the blue saying that they raped or forced themselves on them." But the truth of it was that I put myself in a terrible situation. When Nicole told me she was married, I should have moved on. She did what she wanted to do with me, as God is my witness. She was probably lonely, missing that connection with her husband, and got caught up in a mixture of the loneliness and excitement surrounding the show. After she slept with me, her guilt must have been too overwhelming for her, and she had to justify her actions to her own self. Like Jamie Foxx said in his song, "Blame it on the alcohol."

*Hanging with the troops at Al Dahafra US Air Base
in the United Arab Emirates in 2005.*

20
London Calling

London, England

While returning home from our three weeks in the sand entertaining the troops in the Middle East, we had a three-hour layover at London's Heathrow airport. What do you do for three hours in an airport? The other comedians and I killed time by walking around and checking out the place. As I was walking around the airport, I walked into to a high-end store and ran into Monica. Monica was a five-foot-six-inch beautiful sister in her early thirties. She had a sexy body, a rock star hairdo with brown highlights, and a nice, round African ass. She also had a British accent that sounded ultra cool. It was good to talk to someone who sounded stranger than me when they talked. Initially, when I started talking to Monica, she didn't seem too interested. Then when I told her I was a comedian living in Los Angeles, she came alive. Just when our conversation was heating up, there was some kind of fire alarm going off in our section of the airport, so all the customers and passengers had to exit the store and go to a quarantine area until everything was deemed okay. Before I cleared out, I gave her my business card and told her to give me a call if she was ever in Los Angeles. By the time the drill was over, it was time to catch my flight back to Cali, so I didn't get a chance to see Monica again. I didn't really think I would hear from her, so she faded out of my mind.

Three months later I'm sitting in my apartment and the phone rings. When I answered it, I heard a distinctive female voice on the other end with a British accent. It was Monica, and she was telling me she planned to come to Los Angeles to visit in the late part of summer. For the next few months, Monica and I talked every day on the phone. Because of the eight-hour time difference, we did most of our talking in the evening. During these many conversations, I learned that Monica was born in Jamaica but moved to England when she was a little girl. Her mother lived in New York, and she had visited her a few times. She'd been married for seven years but didn't have any biological kids of her own. Her husband had a set of twin daughters that she pretty much raised as her own, but once they got divorced, he took them with him and she never saw them anymore.

She talked about her biological clock ticking and eventually having kids of her own. She wanted to move to America and have her kids here because of all the benefits the kids could grow up with. However, before she could move to America, she would have to get her green card because she never bothered to get one back when her mother suggested it ten years earlier. When she was married she never thought she would want to live in America because she had everything she wanted. Then September 11, 2001, happened and Homeland Security tightened the rules for entering the country, and she was stuck. It was going to be more difficult for Monica to move to America now without lining up all of her ducks in a row and getting all of her paperwork in order. But I told her these were all things we could discuss when she got to Los Angeles.

After several months of daily phone calls, e-mails, and exchanging photos via e-mail, Monica finally arrived in sunny Southern California. When I picked her up at the airport, she looked even more beautiful than I remembered. She was rocking a baby T-shirt, some tight jeans, and shiny black heels. To save on her expenses, I told her she could stay with me for the two weeks she was visiting. It was early in the day when she arrived, so I brought her back to my place so she could freshen up. While trying to pick out something to wear, Monica walked into the living room wearing a thong and a bra to ask me a question. I'm not sure if it was intentional, but it got the room heated up real fast. Next thing I knew, we were down and dirty on my couch. We went at each other for a couple of hours until we fell asleep. By the time we woke up, it was already after 5:00 p.m., so we went at it one more time before getting up, showering, and getting dressed.

Since Monica had never been to Los Angeles before, we did the typical tourist tour. The first thing she wanted to see was the Walk of Fame, so I drove her down to Hollywood Boulevard. We hung out there for a few hours, talking, laughing, and watching the other tourists be tourists before returning to my place. By the time we got home, both of us were horny again, so we got to playing with each other one more time. Monica was a screamer, so I literally had to put a pair of socks in her mouth to keep her from waking up my neighbors whenever she reached an orgasm.

I took Monica everywhere while she was in LA visiting. She liked the Getty Museum up on the hill in Brentwood. She fell in love with the panoramic views of the city from the museum. I could understand it because I loved that view myself and often went to the Getty just to see it more so than the artwork there. Every time I visited the Getty, I envisioned that this was how the rich and famous people who lived in their million-dollar homes in Bel-Air or the Hollywood Hills must feel — on top of the world. I know that was how I always left the Getty feeling.

Another reason Monica enjoyed the Getty was because I used to work there as a security officer, and I was able to give her some personal insight on some of the art and locations while we were touring the museum. I was like her personal docent. Because I used to work at the Getty, I jokingly told Monica that I knew a few hideaway spots where we could go play with each other. Well, she took me up on it. We went down on the P3 level of the South Pavilion and fooled around with each other for a few minutes. There was nothing like a quickie during the early part of the afternoon. I had to tell Monica to make sure to keep her moans and screams to herself or else we might end up on the Internet on some crazy website.

We ate and took pictures while we were there and also lay down on the grass down by the garden and talked quite a bit. She was determined to see everything in Hollywood that she had seen on television or in the movies.

The next day we went to Beverly Hills. Our first stop was NikeTown. One of my buddies, William, worked at one of the big talent agencies that was located directly above the Nike Store, so I stopped by and saw him. I met William when he and I worked as temps at United Talent Agency back when I first moved to Los Angeles, and we've been buddies ever since. William was a thirty-something-year-old, bald-headed brother who was originally from the Caribbean. He was about my height with a real gracious personality. William always went out of his way to make other people feel comfortable. Women loved this about him. All my buddies were nice guys like me. Actually, all my buddies were nicer than me. I have a way of just being abrupt and cold when I get pissed off. William was always diplomatic. He was impressed with Monica from the jump. His girlfriend at the time was from England, so they chatted for a few minutes about the United Kingdom. I told him that Monica loved the finer things in life, so he suggested I take her for a stroll down Rodeo Drive so she could check out what some of the high-end stores had to offer.

Monica and I spent the better part of that day hanging out in Beverly Hills. We ate and caught a movie in nearby Century City afterward. It was a great day but a long one. When we got home, we fell into bed. Even though we were both tired, we found the energy to make love before we fell asleep for good that night. The more I hung out with Monica, the more she grew on me. As the days went by, I learned that

Monica wanted to move to the United States soon and was hoping we'd get more serious — as in married. Even though I liked Monica a lot and she was growing on me, I just couldn't see myself doing that. The situation with Linda, my ex-girlfriend from St. Thomas, ran through my mind and paused any thought I had of repeating an immigrant story. Helping someone start over fresh was hard because they usually didn't know anyone or anything in their new surroundings. As much as I liked Monica, I wasn't sure I could do the "nation building thing" again. Monica was going to require more work and attention than my previous girlfriend who'd moved to Los Angeles to live with me, as she didn't have her immigration papers nor did she know how to drive.

I told Monica that I would let her know my decision before she went back to London. For the rest of the time she was there we continued to go everywhere and do everything together. One night we went dancing; another night we went down to Venice Beach. Going to the beach at night was a hell of an aphrodisiac. Monica had never walked on the beach at night, so we went down to Venice, and sure enough, the hormones started raging. Next thing you know, we're tumbling around on a blanket in the sand, boning. We lay there for a few hours afterward, gazing up at the stars and talking about what-ifs. I knew this: if Monica lived in Los Angeles, we would definitely be a couple. She was definitely hard to resist. Damn! We finally got up and went back to my place in the Valley and went to bed — however, not before we did it one more time. I was the type of guy who liked having sex at least once in the morning and once at night before I went to sleep.

Finally the day came when Monica had to leave to go back to London. On the drive to LAX airport, we talked about what we were going to do. I told her that if she wanted to move to Los Angeles, we could be a couple, but she would have to get her own place. After what I went through with Linda, I'd learned that it was best for the relationship if we both had our own place and gradually got to know each other. Monica wasn't too thrilled about the idea of us living separately, but she said she would think about it. It was a long flight back to England and Monica didn't want to leave. She had really grown on me, and I had conflicted feelings about her leaving, but she needed to go back home because this was getting scary for me. I was starting to fall for someone whom I barely knew. I needed time to clear my head and sort out my feelings.

I stayed at LAX until she went through security and boarded the plane. Then I went home and went to sleep. Monica called me the next day when she landed in the UK. She told me that she already missed me and thought about me all the way back home. I told her that I missed her too and asked her to call me later, after she had a chance to settle in and start her day.

Monica and I talked often on the phone for the next several months. I was supposed to go visit her in London that fall. Most of our discussions centered on her wanting to make a change in her life and move to the United States. I told her that she needed to get her immigration papers fixed before she thought about moving to America and that she should also learn how to drive. She said that it was way too expensive to do both and that it would take over a year to get both things taken care of. She didn't know if she could wait that long. I told her that I still thought we should live in our own apartments if she moved to Los Angeles.

As our conversations continued over the months, Monica started hinting that she had another suitor living in the United States who was willing to move her over to America and set her up. I didn't know if she was trying to make me jealous or light a fire under my ass to make a commitment to her, but I finally told her if she had a deal on the table that was everything that she wanted, she should take the deal because I wasn't planning to budge on my rules. We talked a few more times after that, but I could tell it was over between us. Her phone calls became less frequent, and when she did call, we didn't stay on the phone that long. That was the end of my London lover.

Sitting in the cockpit of F-15 Eagle fighter jet at Al Dahafra US Air Base in the United Arab Emirates in 2005.

21

EL PUMA HERMOSA

Pomona, California

It was a Saturday morning, and I had to drive forty minutes to La Verne, California, to teach a comedy traffic school class. La Verne was approximately forty-five minutes east of Los Angeles. I had to be there by eight thirty to set up and start teaching the class by eight forty-five. I was never a morning person, so I usually would get there, set up the class, and when the first person arrived I'd give them the sign-up sheet, explain the rules, and disappear until nine. Then I would return to my car and pray for a miracle like winning the lottery or getting a call out of the blue from Steven Spielberg offering me a big part in one of his movies so that I didn't have to go back in there and deal with those criminals. Yeah, that's what I called my students, "criminals." I always told them that they were criminals in my class for the next eight hours until they got paroled.

So I didn't get a call from Spielberg nor did I win the lottery. As I sat in the parking lot, I watched some of the criminals walk in, and it looked like a mixed bunch of people. There seemed to be an even mix of men and women attending the class, and some of the women looked attractive too, so that was a plus. Nothing worse than teaching an eight-hour traffic school class stuck with a bunch of men or old people. Talk about a very long day. Those eight hours would feel like sixteen hours. I would rather stay home and watch infomercials all night than torture myself with a class like that. So I went back inside and started my opening spiel, which I call the meet and greet hour. This was where I went around the class and asked each student their name and what they were there for. This really loosened them up and set the tone for the rest of the day.

As I was talking to each student, I finally got to this blonde with a very pretty face and soft voice. I thought she was Caucasian, but I found out later that she was Latin American. Her name was Claudia and she was there for speeding. Apparently after the cop wrote her the ticket, he asked her out. She said no, so there she was on an early Saturday morning spending eight hours with a bunch of criminals too. I told her if the cop had offered to let me go if I went out with him, I would've said yes, given him a fake number, and never thought about him again.

As the day went on, I learned that Claudia got an enormous amount of unwanted attention from men. I also found out that she was single, but her ex-boyfriend would stalk her and continuously call her and bug her about getting back with him. For this reason, I called her Stalkie for the rest of the day. When it was time to pay, I noticed that Claudia (a.k.a. Stalkie) had a slammin' body. She was five feet seven inches, with a butterscotch complexion and a lot of junk in the trunk for a Latina. Claudia was real sweet to me throughout the day. At the end of my classes, I sometimes passed around an e-mail sheet for anyone who wanted to join my e-mail list and come to a future show of mine. I also told them to check out my website. The class ended without much fanfare.

I drove home, ate, and checked my e-mail later that evening. What do you know, Claudia had actually gone to my website and checked it out and joined my fan club through my website. She even sent me a note asking me to let her know about any upcoming shows. She signed it "Stalkie." If I had any doubts as to who she was, that name

Stalkie cemented her in my memory. I sent her a reply e-mail with my phone number. I got a response within fifteen minutes with her phone number in the e-mail, telling me to call her. Since I was at home not doing anything, I called her and we talked for several hours. I had a show coming up that I was producing the following weekend at the HaHa Café in North Hollywood, and I invited Claudia to it. Actually, I sent out an e-mail to all my former traffic school students about my upcoming show, and several of my students RSVP'd that they would be there. Claudia told me she would come if she could get some face time with me after the show. I told her, "Sure." So she agreed to be there.

Saturday rolled around and I did the show. It went great and there was a very good turnout. When I was onstage performing, I thought I saw Claudia in the audience, but I wasn't sure. I also noticed there were several students from my previous classes. When the show was over I stood by the exit and thanked everyone for coming. A blonde lady from my class came up to me and started talking to me. For a minute the way she was speaking, I thought she was actually Claudia because she was saying things about hoping she could get some face time with me after the show and how she thought I was funny and she really liked me. As she was saying these things, I was thinking to myself that I remembered Claudia being much thicker, curvier, and better looking. This lady was skinny, not so attractive, and looked old. Even though Claudia was in her early fifties, she didn't look a day over forty years. She was definitely a hot MILF. Just when I was starting to wonder how I was going to weasel out of this thing with the fake Claudia because I wasn't as attracted to her as I thought, the real Claudia walked out of the club with her friend. Apparently they had stopped to use the restroom and there was a line. Talk about being relieved to see the real Claudia. She walked up and gave me a big hug with that sweet, soft voice of hers. We started chatting. She introduced her friend, who turned out to be her neighbor. I asked them if they enjoyed the show. They both said yes. I offered to walk them to their car and excused myself from the fake Claudia imposter. We made plans to go out sometime in the near future.

The following week, Claudia and I went out to the Yard House Restaurant in Pasadena. We met up at the Ice House Comedy Club. Claudia was looking real sexy that night. She had on some jeans and a top with a pair of heels. She parked her car in the parking structure and then we took my car to the restaurant, which was right around the corner. When we got to the Yard House Restaurant, we ordered drinks and then followed that up with a nice steak dinner. We talked the entire evening. I learned a couple of things about Claudia that night. She was twelve years older than me. She had been married three times, and she had a son in his thirties, who was a millionaire. I also learned that she loved to cook and bake, something I would come to appreciate greatly.

After dinner we drove back to the parking structure to get her car. We sat in the car talking for another thirty minutes. As we were talking I noticed Claudia was getting a little touchy-feely, so I made my move and kissed her. While we made out, I kissed her neck and caressed her breasts. I could tell she was responding to this, so I slid my hand over her crotch and rubbed her fuzzy triangle. Even though she was wearing jeans, I could tell she was getting hot. I placed her hand on my crotch and she stroked it. I quickly unzipped my pants and pulled out Daddy Cool (yes, I am one of those guys who gives his penis a name). I could tell Claudia liked what she was feeling because she kind of stopped, looked, and started going down on me. I thought for sure that I was going to get me some that night, but just when I was starting to enjoy the special attention Claudia was paying to Daddy Cool, she abruptly stopped and said she had to go home. I tried to talk her into finishing what she had started, but she wasn't having any of it. I guessed she figured if she stayed any longer, we were going to end up knocking da boots right there on that first date, so she got in her car and drove home to Pomona. She called me when she got home and told me she made it safely. We made plans to see each other that weekend.

The next Friday night, Claudia invited me over to her place. When I got there, as usual, she was looking and smelling good. I love a woman that looks and smells good. That is a serious aphrodisiac for me. I got there around seven, so we sat around drinking wine, chatting, and watching TV. Claudia loved to drink wine. I learned that night that she used to be a party girl until she had her son. So we sat around drinking and chatting until about ten thirty. That's when things started heating up on the couch. We started kissing, clothes started coming off, and the next thing you know, my face was in Claudia's lap, and she was panting, whining for me not to stop. I ended up tapping it right there on her couch.

After round one, Claudia told me to come into her room, so I followed her in, and as in the case of most women thirty-five and older, her room was her sanctuary. What I mean is, over the years I've noticed that older women's bedrooms were always nicely decorated to their personal touch and scent. There was usually a large bed (queen or king size) with a nice warm comforter and a bedspread on it, along with a bunch of pillows and candles around the room. Claudia's room was no different. When I laid my head in that bed on those comfortable sheets, I almost fell asleep right then and there. But like most women in their forties and older, Claudia was horny, and she wasn't having any of that. I had to perform one more time before I went to sleep, so I woke up and went to work on her again. Claudia climbed on top of me and rode me hard. After she had her orgasm, I got on top of her and finished off the proceedings. I could always tell when Claudia had an orgasm — she always laughed after we were done having sex. At first I thought she was laughing at my performance in bed. It was only later, when she told me what was behind the laughter, that I breathed a sigh of relief. For a minute there, I was thinking the bedroom was the last place a male comedian wanted to receive a laughing ovation.

We fell asleep shortly after that, and the next thing I remember was Claudia waking me up early that Saturday morning, telling me that we had to get up because the cleaning lady was on her way over. I got up quickly and jumped in the shower. By the time I was done in the shower, the cleaning lady was already there and ready to work. I overheard Claudia telling the cleaning lady to start in the kitchen area because her boyfriend was getting dressed in her room. When I first heard this, I started thinking, *I wonder if her boyfriend knows that I was over here?* Then it hit me like a ton of bricks: she was referring to me as her boyfriend. Hmmm. That's another thing I learned over the years — us guys were usually the last to know that we were in a relationship. Oh well, I figured I would address that later. I gave Claudia a big hug and a kiss and left.

After that weekend, Claudia and I saw each other often over the next four years. If we couldn't get to see each other on the weekend, one of us would spend the night at the other person's place during the week. That's another thing I learned over the years; women thirty-five years and older hate to just sit around doing nothing. When they have some free time or a free day, they have to go do something. Claudia was no different. She liked going out and doing things. Whether it was shopping with the girls, brunch with her sisters, a mani-pedi spa treatment, or catching a movie with her girlfriends, she kept her schedule booked. Claudia and I did a lot of things over the time we were together. But no matter what we did or where we went, the night always ended up with us in bed making love. Claudia liked sex a lot, and I was only too happy to oblige her needs.

The more Claudia and I hung out, the more I noticed she loved attention. She was of the mind-set that if I had any free time at all, we should be spending it together. Of course I saw things differently. Before I met Claudia, I had a life and I had things to do even if I wasn't working. This created friction early on in our relationship because she always wanted to be with me and I needed space to do what I had to do, whether it was to perform at an open mic night in LA, hang out with my buddies, or just lay around my place watching TV and talking on the phone. Because we started arguing about my free time, I found myself not always telling Claudia when I had an open weekend.

Which reminds me of a Valentine's Day story. I had a show to do but didn't want Claudia attending because I wanted to hang out with my buddies after the show. I knew if she came, she would want to hang with me, and I just didn't feel up to it that weekend. However, Valentine's Day was that same Saturday night as my show. So in order to do my show in LA without Claudia attending, I told her that my show was out of town. She was crushed when I told her I was going to be out of town for Valentine's Day because she had already planned to spend the day and night with me. I promised to make it up to her.

I had to teach traffic school all day that Saturday, and my show was later that night at the MBar in Hollywood. So to appease Claudia, I had my buddy Big Fran meet me at the location where I was teaching, and he took the gift I had bought for Claudia to her house. (Claudia had met my other buddy Spence, but Big Fran was always cancelling on me whenever Claudia was going to be around, so she started thinking he was my imaginary friend.) He drove the hour or so to her house in Pomona, knocked on her door, and delivered it. Initially when Big Fran showed up at her door, Claudia was a bit skeptical about opening the door for him. I guess it had something to do with him being a strange black man showing up at her front door out of the blue. Big Fran informed her that he had a delivery for her. When she opened the door, he gave her the gift and told her it was from me. A big smile came across her face. She started laughing when he told her who he really was. Her response was, "So you do exist. You're not an imaginary friend of Jeff's."

That was the last Valentine's Day we would share together. Less than a year later, I would eventually tell Claudia that our relationship was over. As much as I liked Claudia, I had to end our relationship. She wanted a life partner, someone to live and travel with. Even though I wanted all of those things too, I just wasn't ready for that with her.

I really dug Claudia though. She was probably the sweetest woman I had ever dated at that point in my life, but the relationship had run its course. I needed to get out while I still could, with my sanity and heart still intact. And if I hadn't ended it, I knew she would have eventually ended it. I just wasn't going to be her guy.

*Signing autographs for the troops after a show at
a US military base in Qatar in 2005.*

22

THE FREAKS COME OUT AT WORK

Santa Monica, California

During the early part of the new millennium, I went back to school to finish my college degree. While I was doing this, I signed up with a temp agency. The agency initially got me a three-week assignment to work at a law firm. This three-week assignment ended up lasting approximately seven years. It was my first time working in a law firm, but it was one hell of a crazy ride.

I started out in the office services department at the firm as a temp. Because I was a temp, I made it a point to keep to myself and not get to know anyone. This way it was easier when my assignment ended to just leave — less people to say good-bye to. But the powers that be must have really liked me a lot, because my three-week assignment turned into a year. The firm wanted to hire me, but I kept resisting. Call it the artist in me, but I didn't want a permanent day job that would prevent me from going to do my auditions and comedy gigs when I booked them. For a while I kept refusing to accept the permanent position in office services that the firm offered me. Then one of the African American secretaries gave me a good piece of advice that made me take the job. Her name was Shannon. She was in her late forties and from the East Coast.

One day while I was delivering a copy job to Shannon, she asked me if the firm had offered me a position. I told her they did, but I didn't want to take the job and tie myself down just in case I got something else on the creative side. Shannon told me that she understood where I was coming from, but she advised me to take the job for the benefits — if a gig or something came up that I just had to go and do, I could always quit the job. Until Shannon told me that, I had never looked at it that way. Yeah, I could always quit, so I signed the job offer papers and turned them in to the human resources department. Two days later, the firm got rid of all its temps in the office services department. Wow, I had just dodged a bullet. I would've have been without a job if I hadn't heeded Shannon's advice. One of the other temps that I had consulted with wanted to hold out for another dollar on his hourly paycheck and was let go with the rest.

Working at the firm was a good thing for me because I had recently decided to go back to college to finish my degree. When I quit going to my classes at the University of Houston in the early 1990s, I hadn't realized that I had enough credit hours to be a senior. A semester or two and I would have had my degree. So there I was back at California State University, Northridge (CSUN), trying to finish and work a full-time job. The firm was really good to me during this time. My bosses allowed me to take my classes in spite of an ever-changing schedule each semester. They allowed me to come in and make my full-time hours. I still got to go and do my comedy gigs whenever they came up. The staff at the firm was cool to me, and I was enjoying life. Things were looking up for me.

One weekend I was producing my Ambassadors of Comedy show at San Gennaro Restaurant in Culver City, and a couple of my coworkers came out to support me. Most of the staff at the firm were females, and I interacted with them on a daily basis. Lisa came with another coworker named Dominique. After the show, Lisa, Dominique, and I started talking about the firm and life in general. Lisa convinced me that I should hire her to work my door for my events. I liked Lisa's spunk.

She was a light-skinned African American sister from Washington, DC. Lisa was very loud and vocal but in a friendly kind of way. I liked her, so I agreed to hire her to work the door at my events and collect the money.

Dominique, on the other hand, was just the opposite. She was a white female in her mid-forties, with shoulder-length black hair and a set of porn star breasts. I didn't know at the time that Dominique was a big flirt, but I would find this out real soon. She had a son who was about eight years old, who danced all the latest hip-hop and street dances. She was telling me how good he was, and I suggested that perhaps he could open my show one of these days. She liked the idea and said we should talk about it more. I gave her my card, and we all called it a night and went home.

Monday rolled around and I got into work around noon. The firm had rented out three floors in a high-end office complex in Santa Monica, so at that time, I was stationed on the third floor. I had my own workstation a few doors down from Dominique's desk, so I knew I would see her before the day was over. She was a secretary who worked for several attorneys. This particular day started out like any other. I went to my classes at CSUN in the morning from eight to eleven thirty. Then I would leave school and drive straight to work. I usually got to work by twelve thirty; right around the time the staff went to lunch. When I got to work, the first thing I did was check into my work area and made sure everything was fine. Then I would go and stick my head into the lunchroom and see what the latest happenings around the firm were.

That day, I saw Lisa in the lunchroom; actually, I heard her before I saw her. This was usually the way it was with Lisa — you heard her before you saw her. When she saw me she started telling everyone about my comedy show the previous weekend and how they should have checked it out. Dominique was in there too. I stayed for a minute and then went back to my work area.

About an hour later, Dominique came by my workstation. She had to get some copies made, so I did them for her. As she waited for her job, she started asking me about my shows and how long I had been performing. She asked me when my next show was, and I told her there was a show scheduled for the following weekend. I asked her if her son was available to do an opening dance number, and she suggested that I come by her place and meet him. I agreed and said that I could do so later in the week. On her way out the door, Dominique grabbed my ass and squeezed it. I didn't think anything at the time because I was flattered by the attention. I should have known better. Sometimes when a person lets certain things slide, they become reoccurring incidents.

For the next several months, whenever I saw Dominique around the firm, she had to flirt with me. If she wasn't trying to kiss me or press her body up against mine, she was grabbing my jewels or my ass. At first it was flattering to get the attention from her because it broke up the mundane chores of my workday. Then I started hearing things around the firm about Dominique and how she hooked up with a lot of men outside the job. At first I didn't know if I should believe the gossip because when you work at any company, the gossip mill is rampant. Then I started hearing things from Dominique's very own mouth and seeing things as well. Like one time I was walking past her desk on my way to deliver a copy job and the way her computer was positioned, I could see her monitor. On her screen, she had naked and semi-naked pictures of men that she was chatting with online. At first, I didn't believe what I saw. So on my way back to my workstation, after dropping off the job, I looked and there it was again — the naked pictures of various men.

Another instance took place during lunchtime. I had just arrived to work from school. After checking in, I went to the lunchroom to get something to drink. Before I walked in, I could hear Dominique talking to someone. I buzzed myself in and proceeded to get something to drink out of the fridge. I don't know if she saw me, but she kept on talking as if she didn't. I just heard part of her conversation, but what I picked up on was enough. She was talking about the throng of guys she had met online. "I met a guy from Texas who's flying in tonight. I'll pick him up when I get off from work tonight. Then when he flies out at the end of the week, another guy I met online from New York is flying in. He's going to stay a couple days with me." She sounded as if she had a buffet of men knocking down her doors to get at her. Initially, I wasn't looking to get intimate with Dominique, but after seeing what I saw and hearing all the things I heard, I damn sure wasn't planning on doing so now.

I really started going out of my way to keep my distance from her, but it seemed like the more I did so, the more Dominique came at me. After a while, it almost became a game of cat and mouse. I would see or hear her coming, and I would turn and go the other way. Because I worked right around the corner from her, it was impossible to totally avoid her. One day she barged into my workstation and got right up on me and in my face. I remember her saying to me, "I've been trying to give you some ass, but you act as though you're scared."

I looked at her and replied, "You have enough batters. You don't need me pinch-hitting!" (Guys like using sports analogies to get their points across. I figured this was a real simple analogy that she would understand.)

She pulled up off me and glared at me with disgust. Then, check this out, she stuck her hand down the front of her spandex pants, fingered herself, pulled it out, and tried to stick it in my mouth. As she was trying to wipe her finger across my lips, she said, "This is what you're missing."

I quickly grabbed her hand and told her, "I do not want your DNA anywhere on my body!"

I must've pissed her off when I said that because she stormed out of my workstation all mad, saying all kinds of crazy stuff and calling me names. "Maybe you can't handle what I have to give or perhaps you're gay!"

For the next couple of weeks, Dominique stayed pissed at me. She would hardly come by my workstation to ask me to do any jobs for her. When she did come by, she refused to speak. That was cool with me because I preferred that we just acted like regular coworkers without all the other crazy stuff. This kind of treatment lasted for approximately a month. Then she reverted back to her old ways, constantly hitting on me. One day she came into my workstation while I was working on a copy job at the machine. I had an open bottle of water on my desk. Dominique picked up the bottle and said to me, "This is what I want to do to your dick." Then she started bobbin' her head up and down on the bottle, simulating oral sex. Another time she came into my station and tried to force a lap dance on me. This woman never ceased to surprise me with how far she was willing to go in an effort to get what she wanted.

I had started confiding in a few female coworkers that I felt safe talking to. Lisa was one of them. I asked her why Dominique acted the way she did. She said Dominique was under the impression that since she was white, all black men wanted her. Wow! That statement shocked me. It was damn sure not true because I didn't want any part of her, especially not with her track record and all the men she was dating. My female coworkers told me I needed to go to human resources and report what she was doing to me. They said they would back me up if I needed witnesses. A couple of my female coworkers had seen or heard a few things Dominique had said and done to me.

At first I just laughed at them. I was like, who was going to believe that I was being sexually harassed by a female? They'd probably laugh me right out of their office. Then as time went on and Dominique kept coming at me, I started to worry about the fallout. She had proven to me that she was capable of holding a grudge when she didn't get her way. I was worried that if I continued to rebuff her advances, she might get upset and storm into human resources and tell them that I'd been sexually harassing her. I hadn't worked in too many corporate offices before, so I really didn't know how I'd be treated if I complained about being sexual harassed by a female. That said, one didn't have to be a rocket scientist to know that the moment a woman accused a man of sexual harassment, his days were numbered wherever he was employed.

Dominique kept up the pressure on me to have sex with her, and as time went by, her mood swings would swing from one extreme to the next. One week she wanted to have sex with me. When I didn't give in, she stopped talking to me and gave me crazy looks whenever I walked past her. This was starting to get too stressful. I constantly worried that she would go to human resources and file a bogus claim against me. The tipping point came one day when she came into my workstation and gave me a job to do. To break up the uncomfortable feeling of two people in the same small space working together, I asked her how her day was going. She just looked at me and said that I needed to leave her alone and quit bothering her. Then she took her job and went back to her desk. That was when I knew she had lost her mind.

The next day when I came to work, I sent an e-mail to the Human Resources Department requesting a meeting. Because the firm was in the process of hiring a new human resources manager, a meeting was set up between me and one of the partners who specialized in human resources cases. In her e-mail to me, the human resources attorney told me to write down a few things about the topic I was coming to see her about. Then she told me she would see me in one hour.

I spent the better part of the next hour trying to remember all the things Dominique had pulled on me. My heart was beating so hard it sounded like a drumbeat. I kept going back and forth as to whether I should just call off the meeting and forget about the whole thing. I didn't want to get Dominique in trouble. I just wanted her to stop, but she didn't seem like she was planning to stop until something happened. Just when I was about to call off the meeting, I got an e-mail from the human resources attorney summoning me to her office. I remember being so afraid of the outcome of the meeting. I hoped that neither one of us lost our jobs; then I hoped that my coworkers didn't look at me as a snitch and subject me to some kind of backlash. I remember thinking, *Damn, how did I get myself in this mess?* I just wanted it all to go away.

When I got to the attorney's office, I walked in and closed the door. She was working on something but asked me what the problem was. I told her that I was getting unwanted sexual advances from a female coworker and wanted them stopped. That was it. I didn't want anyone to get fired. The human resources attorney asked me who the other employee was, and I told her. Then she asked me what kind of things she was doing to me. I proceeded to give her my list of unwanted encounters. She looked at it, and as she was reading some of the offenses, she asked me how long this had been going on. When I told her for over a year, I remember her saying, "A year! That's way too long. We have to put a stop to this ASAP." She picked up the phone and made a few calls. Then she asked me for the names of any coworkers who could verify my claim. I gave her the names of a few female coworkers who had witnessed Dominique in action. Then she assured me that they would get to the bottom of my case quickly. I went back to my workstation feeling bad. I kept beating myself up for diming out Dominique, but I kept coming back to the realization that it was better to report it first and tell the truth rather than allow Dominique to file a bogus claim against me.

When the new human resources manager started work on Monday, he called me into his office that same day and assured me that the firm had already spoken to Dominique and told her to stay away from me. She never bothered me after that. There were times we occupied the same areas of the firm, but she never said or did anything to me. Our interactions were strictly professional.

To this day, whenever one of my buddies brings up my sexual harassment case, they still give me grief. They would say stuff like, "You should've kept your mouth shut and enjoyed the ride." They still can't believe that I actually filed a sexual harassment case against a female. I can't believe it either, but I did it for self-preservation. It was her or me, and I needed the job. The check I received from working at the firm helped pay for the shows I produced. When I looked at the situation through that prism, it was a no-brainer to report Dominique.

*Hanging with the troops at Al Dahafra US Air Base
in the United Arab Emirates in 2005.*

23
RUDE GAL

North Hollywood, California

In over two decades as a stand-up comedian, I am proud to say that I have never been involved with a female comedienne. Not that I didn't want to, because there were a few that I would have loved to sleep with. I always felt that it was tough enough for me to deal with my own highs and lows as a performer, and I didn't need to add to my misery by dating another performer with the same issues. I always steered clear of all the good-looking female comediennes, and I kept our interactions strictly business.

However, there was this one female comic that I sure had the hots for, but I could never figure her out. The first time I met her was at a weekly comedy spot in the Marina area of Los Angeles. It was my first time performing at this location, so I didn't know what to expect. I really didn't feel like performing that night, but I had a female friend (Paula) visiting me from San Diego, so I felt obligated to go out that night and show her around. Paula and I were casually dating. We saw each other whenever we happened to be in the same zip code together. So this particular evening, Paula and I were sitting enjoying an appetizer at the show when Stefanie walked in. From the time she walked into the restaurant and started chatting with Joe, the producer of the show, I noticed her. She was five feet eight inches with thick black hair and an enticing, dusky complexion. The thing that stood out about Stefanie was her smile. Sure, she had a nice physique and a pretty face, but her smile was electric. It literally warmed the room.

Initially I didn't say much to her because I wanted to watch her set to see if she was funny before I seriously approached her. I watched her set, and it was full of observational humor and ethnic jokes that had the crowd roaring. I followed her set with my own. Many of the comics there had never seen me before, so they stuck around to check me out. That night I had a good set, so when I got offstage a few of the comics came up to introduce themselves. That was a comedian's rite of passage. If comics don't know you or have never seen your act, they will be standoffish until they see your act or until one of their friends vouches for you as being funny. Only then will they start talking and joking around with you.

So as the comics were coming up to me introducing themselves, I gave them all my business card and told the ones that I liked and was interested in booking to send me their promo stuff because I produced shows. When some of the other comics who didn't want to talk to me heard that I booked shows, they literally walked over, introduced themselves, and gave me their business cards. I told the comics to e-mail me their promo stuff as I peeked over their shoulders to find Stefanie. I thought she was funny, and I wanted to use her in my comedy group, Ambassadors of Comedy, which featured America's funniest foreign comedians. Stefanie was talking to Joe, the producer, so I went over there and reminded Joe to keep me in his Rolodex and to give me a call the next time he was having a show and needed some comedians. I then turned to Stefanie and introduced myself. I told her that I booked a comedy show called Ambassadors of Comedy and wanted her to be a part of it. She sounded interested and we talked a while. I gave her my business card and told her to send me her promo package. I also told her that she could give me a call sometime. "Okay," she said.

I walked back to the table where my lady friend, Paula, was sitting, paid the tab, and we headed for the side exit. As we got to the car, Stefanie and another male comic walked out talking. She happened to park a couple of cars over from me. She saw Paula getting into my car, and she immediately walked up to me as I was walking back around my car after closing Paula's door. Stefanie then proceeded to ask me, "Is that your girlfriend? Why didn't you introduce us?"

I told her that Paula was not my girlfriend. Then as I got to my car door, I leaned in and introduced Stefanie to my lady friend. "Stefanie, this is Paula. Paula, this is Stefanie." Stefanie stuck her head in the door and they exchanged pleasantries. Then she quickly walked back to her car without saying another word.

As I drove home, between conversations with Paula, I wondered why Stefanie asked me if Paula was my girlfriend. I made a mental note in the back of my mind to inquire with Stefanie about that. I also planned to call up a few of my comic friends to find out if they knew about Stefanie's relationship status.

Stefanie e-mailed me her promo stuff a few days later. By then I had learned that she was single, so I e-mailed her and told her we should catch a movie sometime. She e-mailed me back and said, "Sure. Let me know when."

I replied back in my e-mail, "When is it good for you?"

She replied in her e-mail, "Give me a few days' notice, and I'll let you know when is a good time for me."

I responded, "Cool."

We made plans to see a movie the following week, but I cancelled because I got busy preparing for an unexpected booking. Stefanie and I talked on the phone a few times. She told me that she had been dating an actor, but he didn't want to commit, even though they had been together for over two years.

During one of our early conversations, Stefanie asked me why I didn't have a girlfriend or wife. I gave her my standard reply, "I almost got married but it didn't work out. Now I'm married to my career."

She understood where I was coming from, being a struggling actress/comedienne herself. But she went on to say, "I think you're a player — that's why you've never been married." Truth of the matter was, I never really saw myself as a player because I was always trying to find a girlfriend. I guess deep down I did have a fear of commitment. Looking back now, I see how many great women I let slip away because of my senseless fears.

Over the next few months, Stefanie and I would make tentative plans to go out, but we would never follow through. The timing would always be off for one of us. Needless to say, no horizontal dancing ever happened between Stefanie and me as much as I would have loved it to.

About a year later, I was screening my new short film, *Comedy Traffic School*, at the Ice House Comedy Club in Pasadena and decided to have a show after the screening of my movie. I always wanted Stefanie to perform in one of my events, but like our planned dates, the timing was never right. As I was sitting at my day job dreaming about getting a television deal or winning the lottery, the idea hit me to title my event "Comedy and a Movie." The title was catchy, so it would make it easy to put on a flyer and promote to my fans. I invited Stefanie along with a male comedian whom I wanted to be in the show with me. I called them both up and pitched them the idea. They both loved the "Comedy and a Movie" idea and said they were on board.

The date of the show was a month away, so I had to get everything done before then. I loved producing my comedy shows, but when you're a one-man production company, it was always a lot of stress. I thought my movie was completely done by the time I booked the date for my show. But as it turned out, the director and I had to go back and reshoot a couple of scenes that had technical issues. Then we had to complete the final edits with sound effects and add the music. This was all happening a week before the screening date. We finished the picture the night before the show. The RSVP list numbered one-hundred-plus people, so it was set up to be a raucous night.

Because it was my show, the night of my event I was busy running around like a chicken without a head. I had been producing shows for many years in Los Angeles, so by that time I had a little crew of friends who usually pitched in to help me out. This night I had some of my regulars. Lisa, a crazy but sweet coworker I met from my days at the law firm usually worked my door collecting tickets and checking people in. Big Mike, a thirty-something, unassuming brother I met while working at 94.7 the WAVE, served as a production assistant; and Spence came to cohost the evening. I never went into the showroom when I produced a show because I was usually too nervous and worried about the audience enjoying the show. I normally stayed outside and asked one of my buddies to go and check out the crowd to see how they were enjoying the show. That night was no exception.

While the movie was screening inside in the main room, I was outside talking to Mike and greeting last-minute attendees when Stefanie walked up. She was looking real good that night in some tight black leather pants, a cute blouse, and heels. I walked over and tried to greet her with a handshake. I'm not a big hugger, at least that's what I've been told. Stefanie ignored my handshake and gave me a big hug. Then she started chastising me. "Is this the only way I can see you by agreeing to appear in one of your shows?"

Her comments put me on the defensive. "I tried to take you out but you kept cancelling on me," I shot back at her.

"Yeah, right," she shot right back at me. I showed her the lineup for the show that night; then I told her she was second in the lineup and that the show was going to start after the movie, and I introduced the cast and all that good stuff. Since this was really only my second time meeting Stefanie, I got a sense that she was shy because she just quietly walked into the back of the showroom and sat down.

The comedy section of the show went off with no problems, and afterward we stuck around taking pictures with the fans. I remember walking Stefanie to her car later that evening. We talked about getting together sometime in the near future. Before she drove off, Stefanie gave me another big, warm hug. She had the sweetest scent. In my mind, I was running through the many possibilities of spending some evenings with her.

Again, Stefanie and I did the dance about getting together, but nothing ever happened because we were both busy doing our own things and our schedules kept clashing. It was seven months before I spoke to Stefanie again; I had called to invite her to be in a Valentine's Day show I was producing, and she was down to perform in it. We chatted for a few minutes, and then she told me that she had a new boyfriend. He was rich and thirty years older than her. When she told me that he was so much older than her, I figured she was only dating him for his money. It's LA, so that kind of stuff happened all the time. Now that Stefanie had a boyfriend, a rich boyfriend at that, I figured it was time to cross her off my list of carnal possibilities, at least until they broke up or I started making a whole stack more money than him.

After the Valentine's Day show, another year would pass before I saw Stefanie again. I had created a new live comedy show titled *The Caribbean Comedy Tour*. This show featured comedians born in the Caribbean or descendants of parents born in the Caribbean. I was booking the show in cities with large Caribbean populations. Initially when I created the show, I created it for Gerry Bednob from the movie *The Forty-Year-Old Virgin* and myself. Gerry and I went all the way back to the start of the Ambassadors of Comedy days. Gerry was originally from Trinidad, and me being from the Virgin Islands made us the prefect comedians for the show. *The Caribbean Comedy Tour* show with Gerry and me was called "the Trini and the Virgin." Gerry did one show with me in the beginning. Ever since he appeared in *The Forty-Year-Old Virgin*, he had been staying busy working in movies and television, so I had to quickly find a replacement for Gerry. Stefanie was the first person that came to mind. She agreed, and I changed the title of the show to *The Caribbean Comedy Tour* featuring the Haitian and the Virgin.

Our first show together was in Atlanta. We did a good job, but while we were on the road together, Stefanie kept flirting with me, or at least that's what I thought. She kept making all these sexual innuendos. For example, she was staying at a hotel and I was staying by my buddy's house. When I went to drop her off at the hotel, I walked her to her room and made sure she got in safely. Before I turned to leave, she said, "I have two beds in my room—you don't have to leave." I thanked her but declined and went on my way. Another time she kept telling me how it had been a while since she had sex because of a back injury she suffered in a car accident. Then another time she was telling me how she really liked sex and that doggy style was her favorite position.

All this sex talk made me wonder where she was coming from. I told my buddy Lauren "Ren" Gumbs in Atlanta about Stefanie's musings to me about sex, and he thought it was odd. Ren and I go all the way back to St. Thomas when we were kids growing up. He was a year younger than me, but we were tight ever since junior high school. Ren and I both wondered if she was hinting that she wanted to fool around. I brushed it off to just crazy comedian talk and forgot about it even though she continued to bring up the sex thing periodically.

The next show we did was in Houston and the sexual innuendos continued. She was saying things like "I'm horny," "It's been a while since I got some," "How do you like your sex?" Believe me, I would've loved nothing better than to bend Stefanie over right then and there and do her, but I remembered that she had a boyfriend, and I didn't want to disrespect him. I did start to wonder if Stefanie's boyfriend wasn't servicing her enough in the bedroom. Then I thought that since he was in his mid-seventies and she in her mid-forties, perhaps he wasn't able to sex her down the way she liked it. Whatever the reason for her not getting any sex, I decided that I was going to keep my distance and make sure nothing happened between us.

I survived the tour without anything going down with Stefanie. I was actually relieved to be back in Los Angeles, returning to my regular routine without the hassle of avoiding Stefanie. One day Stefanie called and told me that she was in my neighborhood visiting a friend who wasn't home, and she needed to pee. Being friendly, I offered the use of my bathroom. Stefanie came upstairs and used my facilities. When she came out she proceeded to sit on my couch. We started talking about every and anything. Like most of Stefanie's and my previous conversations, this conversation soon took on a sexual undertone.

First we started talking about comedy. Then we moved on to places to find a job. While I made suggestions about places to find a job, Stefanie started making comments about being sleepy. I told her she could lie down on the couch if she wanted to, and I gave her a pillow and comforter. As she lay down on the couch and got comfortable, she said, "I normally don't wear clothes when I'm inside my place."

I told her, "Don't let me stop you if you wanted to get naked." As I said this, I was thinking, *Is she really going to get naked? Is she trying to tell me to make a move on her by suggesting she wanted to get naked?* It wasn't like it was hot. It was the fall, so I knew she wasn't burning up. I always hated when a woman hinted about things and didn't come right out and tell me what exactly was on her mind. I was the worst when it came to trying to read a woman's mind. Oh well, I just shrugged it off.

We talked some more about comedy. Then Stefanie started making hints about needing some money to pay her rent. I finally asked her about her rich boyfriend and why he wasn't giving her what she needed. Stefanie proceeded to tell me how her boyfriend was more talk than action. The money he supposedly had, she had yet to see any of it. Then I said, "You've got to know quite a few guys with money who want to date you."

She replied, "Yes, but guys with money usually want you to blow them or have sex with them just for dinner or a couple drinks. I'm not doing that!" Then she went on to say, "I wish I knew a couple of rich guys in Las Vegas that wanted to have sex with me. I would charge them five thousand dollars each." Then she looked at me. In my head

I was wondering what the hell she was talking about. Was she hinting to me that I could have sex with her for money? If that was the case it wasn't going to happen. I would have loved nothing better than to jump between Stefanie's thick, juicy thighs, but I wasn't going to pay to do so. No way, Jose!

Then Stefanie started talking about how she had refused to have sex with her boyfriend until he gave her some money. Next she started telling me about some new guy she met recently and how she spent the night over at his place the previous night. She told me that as she walked through his front door, she took off all her clothes, and they spent the night having sex. As she told me all this, I was thinking, *Where the heck is this conversation going? Why is she telling me all of this? Is she trying to get me to make a move on her or what?* I needed to get out of there for a minute, so I told her I was running to the post office to mail something and she could stay until I got back. She said, "Okay." I grabbed my keys and left.

On my way to the post office, I called my buddy Ren in Atlanta and told him what was happening. He kept laughing at me all the way there and back. He told me that she probably wanted to have sex with me but didn't want to be the aggressor. I told him that I would let him know what happened as I arrived back at my place.

When I got back inside my apartment, Stefanie was sleeping. I was a little relieved to see that she hadn't gotten naked. I was doing my best to show restraint and not give in to my urges. I knew if I got involved with Stefanie sexually, it would mess up our business relationship. Stefanie woke up shortly after I returned, and she kept saying that she was hungry. I wasn't sure if she was hinting for me to take her out to dinner or not. I was getting horny, and I wasn't sure what Stefanie's motives or her intentions were, so I started feigning sleep. I hoped her friend would come home soon and she would have to leave, saving me from having to make a move on her. Besides, I didn't really want to start anything sexual between us because things could get messy down the road. Stefanie tried calling her friend a few more times with no success. She left shortly after that, and I breathed a sigh of relief. I couldn't figure out what her intentions were, and I didn't want to make a move only to find out it was the wrong one and have Stefanie hold it against me forever. I wished most women would just say what it was they wanted and quit making men try to read their thoughts. We aren't mind readers. At least I'm not anyway.

*Onstage at Cal State Sacramento in 2010 performing
with my comedy group, Ambassadors of Comedy.*

24

WTF!

Cumberland, Maryland

I got booked to do some more one-nighters on the East Coast during the late spring and early summer months. Obama had recently been sworn in as the first African American president of the United States, so I was feeling good. America was moving forward. I flew in to Washington, DC, rented a car, and drove to my first stop, Cumberland, Maryland. I had never performed in Cumberland, but the booker said it was a good gig. The show was at a local bar that had comedy once a week. Like most one-nighters, the pay was crappy, but I wasn't doing it for the pay — I was doing it for the road experience. You can't teach a comedian all the things he'll learn while performing on the road.

As was customary when I went on the road, the first thing I did upon arriving in a new town was to drive to the motel and check in. Then I drove by the club where the show was being held and checked out the surroundings. I wouldn't go inside; I would just drive by so I would know how to get to the place. There wasn't much to do in Cumberland, so I went back to my room and watched cable television for a few hours. Later, I went over my set list for the show that evening. Then I took a nap for a few hours. When I woke up, it was already getting dark, so I took a shower and got dressed. Showtime was at eight-thirty that night, so I left my room at eight o'clock. The drive was less than five minutes, so I got to the club in no time.

When I walked into the club, I looked around and checked out the audience. Like most of the clubs I performed in, I was the only black person around, but that fact didn't bother me. I was used to it after all these years of performing. It was a two-man gig. I opened up the show. I went up onstage, did my thing for thirty minutes, and got off. The crowd responded well to me. The headliner went up and did his forty-five-minute set and got off the stage. He had a good set too. Because there wasn't much to do in Cumberland, the headliner and I stuck around the club interacting with the patrons.

While I was hanging out and chatting with the bar patrons, I started up a conversation with a lady named Wendy. Wendy was an attractive lady in her early thirties. She was real friendly and pretty much hijacked my time for the rest of the night. She had come to the show with her husband, John. John was an average-looking guy, the type of dude who collected a paycheck at a job he hated, came home, ate dinner, and went to bed. He was fairly short, slight, and sported a thick mustache and beard. He didn't say much; he was the opposite of Wendy's perky personality.

As I was sitting chatting with them, a song that I liked came over the speakers and I excused myself to hit the dance floor. A few seconds later, Wendy joined me. I asked her about her husband's whereabouts. She said, "He doesn't like to dance." I just shrugged my shoulders and kept dancing, and Wendy started dancing with me. Now I wasn't trying to get in the middle of anything, but I didn't own the floor or the music, so what could I really do? We danced to a few songs. Then we went back to our seats and talked some more. Actually, Wendy started talking to me some more. John just sat there pounding his beers. Occasionally, he would get up and go to the restroom or to talk to some friends he saw. Wendy and I would periodically go to the dance floor whenever we heard a song that we liked. We kept this up till the club closed down at 2:00 a.m.

I was all set to go back to my room and watch a little television until I fell asleep. Then as Wendy, John, and I were walking out the door, Wendy suggested that I come over to their house and hang out for a few hours. She assured me that she didn't have to work the next day. At first I declined but Wendy insisted. She said that they just lived right across the border in West Virginia, and it wouldn't be a problem at all. By this time, John had gone to get their car, and I asked Wendy if her husband would be okay with me coming over this late. She replied, "Of course he will." Then she continued, "Just follow us. It's right up the street."

I was a little skeptical about going over to a stranger's house so late, but I wasn't sleepy, and Wendy seemed like a really nice person, which helped alleviate my concerns. So I jumped in my rental car and followed them. Wendy was right; they literally lived just up the street from the club on the other side of the border in West Virginia.

Their house was on a hill lined with older but tidy houses. I parked on the street, and by the time I got out of my car, Wendy was standing in the doorway with the door wide open waiting for me. As I walked in, I asked Wendy where her husband John was. She closed the door and responded that he had to go to work later that morning, so he was in their room lying down. Then she went to fix me a drink. While she was in the kitchen I looked around the house. It was a one-story, three-bedroom house — very clean and very cozy.

Wendy returned from the kitchen with my drink and then sat down next to me on the couch. I picked up our conversation from where it left off at the club. As we sat there chatting in the living room with the TV playing in the background, I noticed that Wendy had changed into shorts and a T-shirt. I also noticed that she was sitting real close to me on the couch. My mind started to drift and think crazy thoughts, but I stopped it before it got too far. I really wasn't looking for trouble, but I was beginning to suspect that Wendy might be feeling me. I quickly shot that thought down because her husband was in the next room lying down. There was no way she would think about doing anything with me with her husband so close. Besides, I had made a promise to myself before I left home that I was going to abstain from any kind of sexual contact while I was on this road trip. I wasn't about to break that promise now, especially not with some married lady, and risk getting myself killed in the process. I was firm in my conviction and determined not to give in to my demons. We continued chatting, and after about an hour, Wendy excused herself to go check on her husband.

While I was waiting for her to come back, I started watching TV. I could hear the faint vibrations of an intense conversation going on in the bedroom. It sounded like Wendy and her husband were having a disagreement about something or another. The more I listened, the more I realized the disagreement was about me. Then the discussion started moving closer. Wendy and John had walked from their bedroom into the kitchen. John's voice was rising while Wendy seemed to be trying to keep the level of the discussion down so I couldn't hear. Without warning, I heard John yell, "I don't want any nigger in my house!" Whoa! I had never heard a Caucasian person use that word in my presence before, and to make matters worse, I had never had the word "nigger" directed at me.

When I heard that, I jumped up off the couch and started heading for the door. Before I reached the door, Wendy had already beaten me to it. She began apologizing for her husband's actions. Just then, John came out of the kitchen, red faced, and he too was apologizing profusely for what he had just said. He said he wasn't a racist and that it had just slipped out. Isn't that what all the racists say? He blamed it on all the alcohol he had drunk earlier that evening. He said that I could stay as long as I wanted to and that he was going to go back to bed. Both he and Wendy were urging me to stay, but I looked at my watch and it was already going on four o'clock in the morning. I told them that I had to get up early to drive to my next gig. I literally ran out to my car.

As I was driving off, I could hear Wendy and John arguing again. She was screaming at him for running me off with his racist comments. He was yelling at her for flirting with me. As I was driving to my room, I started having all kinds of visions of scenes from the movie *Mississippi Burning*, where racist white folks were attacking black people. I kept thanking the Lord for watching over me that night and making sure nothing tragic happened. Most of all, I thanked him for allowing me to resist my urges and to be strong in my convictions. I was finally starting to see light at the end of the tunnel for me.

*Hanging with my buddies after a show at The MBar in Hollywood,
California, 2010. Left to right: Loni Lee, Cedrick "Hollywood"
Robinson, Francis "Big Fran" Acquaye, Denver "Spence"
Williams, Mike "Big Mike" Jackson and me (center).*

Looking Back

Yeah, I've been through a lot of things over the years. Now I don't want anyone to think that I don't recognize the part I played in my misadventures. I was present and a part of everything that happened along the way. And I'm not saying I would advise some soon-to-be young man to follow my example. Every woman I have dealt with was a new experience, and I have a lot of them to talk about. Some of them were funny, others not so much, but all in all I have to own my place at the table of those experiences.

The truth is I have always wanted love. I just didn't know how to accept it, how to make it work, or how to keep it in those rare moments when it came knocking. I look back now and see so many possibilities for happiness that I let pass me by because of my own issues. The good thing is that experience is a good teacher. All these years and all those chapters in my book have led me to where I am now. A man, a father, a comedian looking to be better in all of those roles while leaving my heart open for real love.

These days I am looking at women differently than I have in the past. I'm seeing them through my actions. How am I coming off? How am I interacting with them? Am I making myself available, not just physically but emotionally? I would love my next book to be about the life of a successful comic and how he navigates his career with his marriage. And I would talk about how hard it is to leave home to go on tour. I would talk about how warm I felt knowing the tour was coming to an end and I would be flying home to eat breakfast with my wife, at our kitchen table. And make love all day long. See you at the club ...

The Poem
Hollywood, California

A female friend of mine, who hung out with me in the late 1990s, wrote this poem about me. I like it because she was one of the few people who were able to capture the true essence of what Jeff Hodge was about in every sense of the word.

19 to 20—Hanging Out with Mr. Hodge

M. Davis

Picked up the phone and dialed your number,
Listening to the ring, waiting in anticipation,
Thinking and planning the message I'll leave on your voice mail.
But you pick up and say, "Hello."

You're off to do a show and I smile:
Two different paths taken.
Found a tape you made,
Listening to the sound of our friendship.

Songs that took me back,
Back in time to your '86 Honda Accord.
Listening to you get pumped playing 2Pac,
Speeding up the 110 Freeway, late as usual.

You've got a show to do,
Pulling up to the Ice House Comedy Club.
Listening to your jokes, rolling my eyes,
As you schmooze the crowd.

Sitting in the back,
Watching as you tear apart the front row.
Wondering if I will ever end up in your act,
The night is over.

You say, "Let's go, kiddo."
I say, "Okay, old man."
As we laugh at Watermelon and Larry,
Was that his name or what?

Running around,
Yeah that's what we did.
I was in the background; You were in the show.
I was your entourage. Maybe that's a bigger metaphor for my life.

As I sat back and marveled at your beauty,
You pushed me.
As the year passed, I grew up.
One day at a time, I moved past my rose-colored dream.

So I picked up my stuff and walked out the door;
That was the end of our romantic endeavor.
Time passed;
I called to see how you were doing.

We chat for a while,
But now we talk about new loves.
And share old stories and jokes,
A hug and we go our own way.

Just so you know,
If I never get the chance to tell you face-to-face,
That my life, nineteen to twenty,
Your face marks that year.

I still love you.
I know that your heart is easily broken.
Your beauty,
Is so much deeper than your skin.

I've seen your inner torment,
The demons you rustle with.
Like I said I still love you,
So I snuggle up close to your rough exterior.

I smile because I know,
That I'm just a name in your Rolodex.
But you are a larger-than-life character,
In the play that is my life.

So I laugh as I sit,
Listening to the songs
Of our friendship,
Remembering who you were.

When I darkened your doorsteps,
The bed I nagged you to buy;
The comfort you gave me,
When I was so unsure of myself.

If there ever comes a day,
When you feel a little unsteady,
I'll be here for you to reach out to,
With a steady hand and to point you in the right direction, my friend.

About the Author
Comedian/Actor/Producer/Author

Jeff Hodge, a native of the US Virgin Islands, has been called a poor man's Tyler Perry because he acts, produces, writes, and does stand-up comedy. Since getting into comedy two decades ago, Jeff has accomplished many things, including appearing in the feature films *Deuce Bigalow: Male Gigolo, Crocodile Dundee in LA*, and the television sitcom *The Jamie Foxx Show*. Jeff can be seen from time to time in his recurring role as different characters in sketches on *The Tonight Show*, hosted by Jay Leno. Jeff has opened for world-renowned saxophonist David Sanborn and comedians George Lopez and Arsenio Hall and has written material for *The Steve Harvey Radio Show, Arsenio Hall, George Lopez*, and *The Keenen Ivory Wayans Show*.

Jeff has authored several successful relationship books, including the very popular *101+ Ways to Keep a Man, 101+ Ways to Tell When the Relationship Is Over,* and *101+ Ways to Tell If the Person You're Dating Is Crazy*. Other books by Jeff include the successful humor books on driving: *101+ Ways to Get Out of a Traffic Ticket, Pet Peeves: Things That Tick Me Off about Driving,* and *101+ Ways to Stay Awake When on the Road*. For more information on Jeff's books, visit www.101waystokeepaman.com.

When Jeff is not onstage performing or writing books, he can be found producing one of his many projects. Recent projects included cowriting, producing, and starring in the short film *Kindergarten*, which was based on a funny incident involving Jeff's five-year-old son. Jeff has also produced and starred in the comedy short *Comedy Traffic School*, which was screened at several film festivals across the United States.

Jeff has also produced a few live comedy shows, including the Ambassadors of Comedy, which features America's funniest foreign comedians (www.ambassadorsofcomedy.com). *The Caribbean Comedy Tour,* a show featuring Jeff and a few of his friends who are comedians from the Caribbean is one of Jeff's latest projects. Last year, Jeff returned from an eight-city USO Tour of the Middle East, where he entertained tens of thousands of troops from all branches of the United States Military and other coalition forces.

Jeff's humor comes from his perspective--—the trials and tribulations of a foreigner living in the United States. So even if you cannot remember what island Jeff is from, after seeing his act you will sure agree with the journalist who wrote, "the bottom line is, he's funny."

www.jeffhodge.com

OTHER BOOKS BY JEFF HODGE

101+ Ways to Keep a Man ($15). A how-to guide instructing women about how men think and what they really want in a relationship. Real-life relationship advice in an easy-to-understand-and-execute manner.

ISBN: 0-595-37633-9

101+ Ways to Tell When the Relationship Is Over ($15). A how-to guide that offers insight into the mentality of some of the things men do when they are no longer interested in being in a relationship.

ISBN#: 0-595-42567-4

101+ Ways to Tell If the Person You're Dating Is Crazy ($15). A how-to guide instructing women how to tell if the person they are dating is mentally stable. Real-life relationship advice in an easy-to-understand-and-execute manner. Even if you are not in a relationship, this book offers some of the telltale signs on how to spot a potentially unstable person that you may be considering dating. It is sure to help you to avoid individuals that may be more wrong for you than right.

ISBN: 978-1-44010-695-8

101+ Ways to Get Out of a Traffic Ticket ($15). A humorous book filled with lots of funny excuses and stories motorists have used over the years to get out of traffic tickets.

ISBN: 0-9633347-0-0

Pet Peeves: Things That Tick Me Off about Driving ($15). A humorous book that shows motorists how to deal with their pet peeves and road rage when they are behind the wheel.

ISBN: 0-9633347-5-1

101 Ways to Stay Awake When on the Road ($15). A humorous book that has funny takes on road signs and what they mean. It also gives readers creative ways to stay awake when they find themselves falling asleep behind the wheel.

ISBN: 0-9633347–1-9

Yeah Mon Entertainment
P.O. Box 88304
Los Angeles, CA 90009
323-359-5569

www.yeahmonentertainment.com

Email: yeahmonentertainment@gmail.com